THE CREATIVE FORAGER

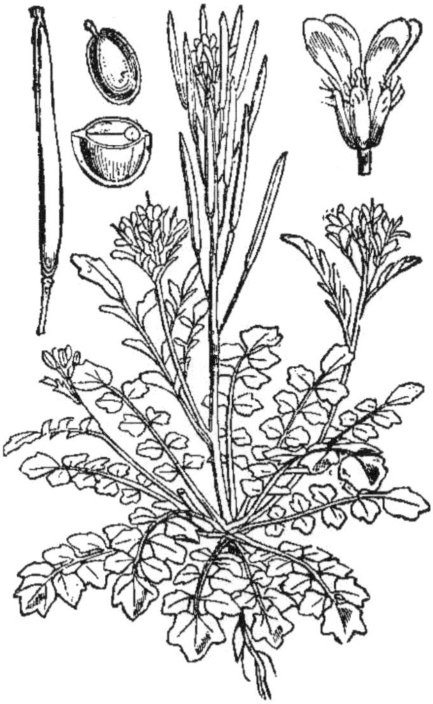

How to Cook with Wild Foods

Presented by INVIRONMENT

Written by Jeremy Puma
with contributions from Tim Boucher

CONTENTS

ACKNOWLEDGMENTS

Thanks to Anthuor and All of the Spirits

Part One:

Foundations of Wild Cuisine

1 INTRODUCTION

This is not a "plant ID" book. There are dozens of those available for the earnest student of foraging (we recommend Thomas Elpel's *Botany in a Day,* coupled with a quality guidebook which covers the plants in your region). **Instead, this is a book about how to *use* wild plants in the kitchen.**

If you're reading this book, you are likely already interested in foraging. You also realize that food is everywhere. If you know where to look, you can find nutritious food in lots of places you might not expect to see it. The question then becomes, what can I do with this, beyond making a salad?

When you start eating wild plants you start seeing potential everywhere.

You start thinking: can I eat that? How can I cook with that? Is there anyone else as crazy as me who I can hook into this strange, yet utterly obvious discovery?

What was once hidden (occult) in plain sight, is revealed, as in that apocryphal gnostic Gospel of Thomas saying, 113:

> *Rather, the kingdom of the father is spread out over the earth, and people do not see it.*

Many of the plants we discuss in this little missive aren't generally "cultivated." Instead, you'll find them in the liminal: between the vegetables in your garden, in empty lots or abandoned spaces, off the path in your local park. These are often plants considered, in common parlance, to be "weeds."

What, exactly, are weeds, anyhow? Are they unwanted plants? If so, the worst "weed" in my yard is the grass in my front lawn—I'd rather be growing food there. Are they "invasive" species? This discounts their potential role in the community of your local ecosystem. The concept of a "weed" is simply a state of mind, and many of the plants we consider "weeds" are actually healthful and delicious.

These plants are "wild," in the sense that they just "happen" without the need for our involvement. Regardless of whether they pop up in your yard or you find them next to the trail on a hike, they present themselves to you, saying take, eat, enjoy.

Those of us who enjoy cooking know that once you've learned some basics, cookbooks become more like books full of *suggestions*. Once you know, for example, that cooking iceberg lettuce and cooking cabbage will yield incredibly different results, even though they look fairly similar, you'll never forget it.

What, then, do you do with dandelions or hairy bittercress? This volume hopes to provide you with some answers.

The essays and recipes in **Part One** present the reader with a foundational understanding of the joy of incorporating wild plants into regular culinary rotation. Chapter 6, "**Wild Edibles: Culinary Keys**," provides the curious cook with a roadmap to using wild foods in the kitchen.

In **Part Two**, we present plant profiles for some very common wild foods which can be found throughout much of North America. These profiles are intended to give the reader a deeper appreciation for what can be found underfoot.

Hopefully this book will open your eyes to a new way of thinking about—and preparing—wild plants, and will allow you to begin participating in your local biosystem in new and interesting ways.

2 VOLUNTEERING AT THE SOIL SEED BANK

Nature abhors a vacuum, and newly bare soil is a good example of Nature's in-built recovery process. When a patch of ground experiences a disturbance (i.e., when you shovel away the top layer of soil or rip out vegetation), it won't be long before weeds begin to sprout.

Why? Where do these weed sprouts come from? I didn't plant any weeds here. Did you?

The soil seed bank is a collection of all of the seeds dormant within the soil in a given locale. They could have come from anywhere: from plants which grew there in the past and dropped their seeds in this area or from plants in other places who seeds were dispersed by wind, water, animals and other agents (including humans).

Seeds from different plants can remain viable in the soil seed bank for variable lengths of time. They say that *Chenopodium album*, lambsquarters, or fat hen, (one of my favorites) can remain viable for anywhere from 40 years on average to potentially up to 1,600 years. I don't know about you, but the idea of eating wild edible plants that grew from centuries old seeds trips me out.

These dormant seeds in the soil seed bank, some of which may be very very old, germinate when exposed to the right conditions. Generally that is following a disturbance—topsoil has been stripped away, seeds are suddenly exposed to water and light, etc. They may not just be weeds either that sprout on up out of the soil seed bank; your garden plants from previous years, or those of previous occupants, may have also added their genetic material to the soil seed bank.

This is where so-called "volunteers" come from—useful plants from previous garden incarnations which show up in unlikely places. They can be a welcome addition to any garden. And so can wild edible plants—"weeds"— once you know which ones are appropriate for human consumption, and which ones fit your personal flavor palette and bioregion, and lifestyle. When you get down to it, weeds are volunteering too. Part of their ecological role is to enable succession to take place: re-covering bare soil, adding nutrients and organic matter to the soil and creating the conditions for other plants to move in and a balanced, integrated ecosystem to form or re-assert itself.

In my garden this year in Québec, I have intentionally stocked the soil seed bank with species that I want to become my nouveaux weeds—the ones I actively want to grow, reproduce and become naturalized over successive generations. Let's develop a self-perpetuating "volunteer" community of beneficial plants: some with a heritage of cultivated genetic material adapted to the place through self-selection, growing alongside plants which have themselves chosen or which Nature has chosen to grow in that place. I will let the weeds grow alongside the volunteers, transplants and other garden additions and invite them all to stay a while and see what develops. In the end, which ones will be weeds?

--- Tim Boucher, Spring 2016

3 WHAT IS A "FORAGER," ANYHOW?

Let's begin with the standard "dictionary definition." This comes from Etymology Online (https://www.etymonline.com/word/forager):

> ***forager (n.)***
> *late 14c., "a plunderer," from Old French foragier, from forrage "fodder; pillaging" (see forage (n.)). From early 15c. in English as "one who gathers food for horses and cattle."*

I can't think of anything less descriptive of the process of recognizing the edible and medicinal value of uncultivated plants, and the process of harvesting them by participating in their ecology, than "plundering," or "pillaging," or "gathering food for horses and cattle." Right?

And to be honest, the word "forage" itself still makes me think of something done primarily by odd, understory-dwelling lemur creatures who give no though to preparation or delight of what they harvest, who "forage" just as a matter of subsistence, to keep from dying, and nothing more. I'm with Euell Gibbons when he said:

> *You can't expect someone to remember a plant when you say, "There's something you can eat as an alternative to starvation." How much better that individual will remember if he incorporates a wild fruit or vegetable into his food right now and finds that he actually likes it.*

Some have suggested "gathering" as an alternative, as in "hunter/gatherer." That's fair; however, it has its own disagreeable connotations. "Gather," to me, implies that the plants being collected just dropped out of heaven like manna and are sitting around in the park for you to go put in a basket. In a way this is true, but I think this negates the effort it takes to learn about non-cultivated edibles, from IDing to preparation to going out and getting them when the time is right.

Of course, neither of these terms irks me, personally, as much as "wildcrafting." The very word implies that one is dealing primarily with "wild" plants, a problematic concept when you really start looking into it. Can you "wildcraft" using weeds from your garden? What about plants from a local urban park? If you intentionally plant some salal on your property and let it "run wild," are you still "wildcrafting" if you harvest the leaves and berries?

What does "wild" even mean?

Is something "wild" because it's never been influenced by humans? If so, nothing is wild any longer—in the Anthropocene Era, we've been influencing the global climate since we started burning stuff in our agricultural fields. If you go into the "wild" on the Eastern Seaboard of the US, or parts of the Interior West, you're going to be in forests almost entirely planted by humans.

Is something "wild" because no humans have ever been there? If so, that leaves very few almost entirely inhospitable places "wild." There are dozens of lists of "Least Explored Places" on the internet, but note that, in most cases, "Least Explored Places" means "Least Explored by White Europeans." I'd bet the indigenous peoples of the Amazon basin and Papua New Guinea would find the placement of their traditional homes on these lists a little laughable. If this is the meaning of "wild," then how does one even "participate" in it?

Is something "wild" because no humans go there very often? If so, we're going to have to include vacant lots and a large part of the suburbs in Detroit "wild."

So do we go with "natural" instead? If so, how do we decide something is "natural"? Is it "something made in nature"? If so, there is very little that's "natural" about any kind of farm, including organic farms.

It's sort of a slippery slope, this conversation about what's actually "natural" and what isn't. And it's just started...

Is it "something made with natural products?" This doesn't work either. Let me give you an example: I know you're likely not terribly keen on plastic, but plastic were mostly made of plant resins for a long, long time. Now they're mostly made using petrochemicals. Petrochemicals are derived from fossil fuel sources. Fossil fuels mostly come from millions-of-years old dead trees. So, plastics are derived from plants. Does that mean they're "natural"?

I want to circle back around to "wild." A lot of what I'm personally interested in fits into the umbrella of "wildcrafting," which is using "wild" or "uncultivated" plant or animal material to create products. If

I'm using nettles I harvest from the local park, which although uncultivated are certainly "managed," does this count?

Or, what about a hawthorn tree that's being used as an ornamental? Say it's also at a local park, but was almost certainly planted intentionally as it's part of a landscape feature. If I make hawthorn jelly using its berries, am I "wildcrafting"?

What if I make an pesto using the chickweed I have in my own garden bed? I didn't plant it, but the soil and water it gets are definitely due to the influence I had over it. Is it "cultivated," or does this count as "wildcrafting"? I don't know!

Look, when you have so many blurred lines, eventually everything will run together, and I think what is ultimately being illustrated here is that all of these definitions consider humans outside or external to the ecosystem. I would like to see more of a blurring of lines based on the idea that humans are intrinsic to the ecosystem, and just because we're less physically present or influential in a place doesn't mean that place is somehow "better" or "more valid."

I'm not sure what this would look like, but for me, ecology happens in a so-called "urban" environment just as readily as in a "wild" environment, and interacting with the weeds and plants that grow in the local park is just as "valid" as interacting with those in the back-country. **Let's face it: we all live in the "wilderness." We just happen to have participated in that wilderness in different ways.** There is no good answer for what a forager actually *is*, but one of the best reasons to forage for wild edibles is that it underlines this process of fully immersing yourself in your local biosystem.

This is a philosophy to which we refer as "Participatory Ecology."

4 MANIFESTO FOR A PARTICIPATORY ECOLOGY

Does any of this sound familiar?

"TEN REASONS TO ESCAPE TO NATURE"

"GET BACK TO NATURE THIS WEEKEND!"

"25 INSPIRING NATURE QUOTES TO MAKE YOU WANT TO GO OUTSIDE AND EXPLORE NATURE"

"It's time to get out in nature and explore the places you are helping protect."

The implication, of course, is that Nature is something Other, something we don't participate in unless we GO to it. This isn't, however, the case. We absolutely NEED to see NATURE as something in which we already participate.

Same shit, different biosystems, all Nature.
Public Domain Images via Unsplash.com

Nature isn't just a collection of biosystems outside of your house; it's a **process** in which entities participate.

Nature is an "exchange of goods and services" via a network of nodes and connections.

Saying "Escape to Nature" is meaningless. It's like telling an octopus to "Escape to the Sea," or a bear to "Escape to the Forest." It's like telling a variable to "Escape to an Algorithm."

You don't need a tent or hiking boots or a long drive to the "middle of nowhere" to experience Nature; the fact is, you can't NOT experience Nature.

What does this mean, exactly? **It means there is no "Wild" versus "Urban."**

It means that the value of entities isn't in the entities themselves, but in the connections and exchanges between them. The better the connections and exchanges of mutually beneficial services in a system, the more value that system has. Valuable Systems—be they forests, cities, workplaces, rivers, the 'soil food web'—consist of entities working together to benefit all of the individual parts of the system.

Animals gathering at the water

Taking Nature out of the equation by separating it, framing it as something to "visit," collapses the value function of the System called "Life on Earth."

Understanding "Nature" as something in which we participate, not as an "Other," is a kind of "gnosis"—a revelatory event that changes the way you see and interact with the world.

Those of us who see the value of recognizing the community, of participating in the intricate system of economies and networks that make up our biosphere, face a difficult road. We understand that, for the majority, "going it alone" seems like the easy way. But there are more than a few of us who understand this differently.

Participation in the biosphere isn't always "fun and games." It's not easy to get along with other organisms and species that have different ideas about how to use the resources we all need. Still, a referendum has been held, and the decision is clear. Most humans have voted to exit the environment.

But we have even more bad news, friends. The fact of the matter is, regardless of how you voted, you can't Leave. We're all ultimately stuck here. We can close our eyes, put our heads in the tar sands and pretend that we don't see, know or care what's happening. Act like it's somebody else's problem to solve, fix, cleanup, and that we can simply 'vote' to exit, to walk away from the millions of years of Life Force that has moved inexorably towards the present moment, filling the environment with consciousness and the means to survive.

But we're damned if we do and we're damned if we don't. We're between a rock and another rock, and in between is a bunch of other rocks. And some are on fire....

The thing is though, it could have been a garden, a paradise. Some say it started out that way, and that it was our error, our failure, our pride, our sin that separated us from it. We cant' speak to what happened long ago—and whatever happened, the end result is the same. So, we have to make the most of it.

We hesitate to give anyone advice after everything that's happened. After all the defeats and let-downs we've known—those of us who have kept watch, those conscientious objectors who weary of the war against participation in something larger, who see that no matter what, we will Remain.

But there are truths we've found which can only be seen close to the ground. The dog's eye view. The worm's eye view. The dandelion's view. The truths of the weak, the small, the seemingly powerless. The truths of the soil and streams, the treetops and the layer of needles covering the forest floor. The truths of those who spend their lives getting eaten....

Those truths? Our Birthrights: the right to eat wild food, the right to sit in the sun, the right to not be harassed by poison, or by factory-made mosquitoes, the right to grow plants and collect clean water, the right to walk in the woods.

Our only way forward, and the only way to Make the Ecosphere Great Again, is to Take Back the Planet. And the only way to Take Back the Planet is to recognize that we are all Participants in our Ecology.

We have to start small; the "big guys" and "fat cats" have the cash, and the votes, and the personalities. But, we have something they don't. We have secret weapons passed down to us through the generations by invisible gray-robed elders who fought the same fight, who have always fought the same fight. We have ethics. And our ethics are our arsenal.

Our ethics are key ideals, basic patterns of interaction with the continuum upon which 'wild' and 'urban' fluctuate. These are our guides as we take our stand, and move within the community of Life:

PARTICIPATION. We are all participants in our biosphere, and should participate as fully as possible.

KINDNESS. Acting on one part of the biosphere impacts all other parts. Therefore, do as little harm as possible when interacting with fellow organisms.

EDUCATION. Learn and observe prior to action, think and consider prior to activity.

RESPECT. Every species in a biosphere has the right of self-determination and our actions should impinge upon that right as little as possible.

SUFFICIENCY. Take and leave only what is absolutely needed. Allow the possibility for new growth in the places you walk.

CARE. Act as stewards of all of the places in the biosphere, be they urban or "wild" or in between. Remove the unhealthy and encourage the healthy.

COMMUNITY. Share these ethics with other organisms.

¡Si se puede! We can do it. We don't have a choice. In this, we will vote Remain, regardless of what the Powers believe they have decided for us, and will walk in the sun, and through the forest, for generations.

5 ETHICAL FORAGING

The foundational approach we consider when thinking about foraging participatory ecology, based on the ethics in the previous chapter. How do we think about the best way to harvest wild edibles while minimizing impact on the communities in which they participate? And, how do we use what we collect safely, yet also respectfully?

To this end, there are a few general Rules that I recommend my students follow when collecting and eating wild ingredients. You'll find a number of variations on these rules, but we've distilled them as best we can as follows:

1. **Unless you're 100% sure you know what something is, DON'T PUT IT IN YOUR MOUTH.** This is good advice in general, but doubly-so when you're eating wild foods. Take a class, pick up five of the tons of books on foraging, and make sure you know what you're eating.

2. **Start small and simple.** The plants we introduce in this volume are easy to identify, relatively easy to find, and quite tasty. Don't expect to become an expert forager overnight; instead, pick a few plants and get to know them really well before moving onto those that are more complicated or harder to identify.

3. **Learn as much as you can about the plants you'll be collecting in the context of your local ecosystem, and forage accordingly**. Dandelion grows like crazy in Seattle, so taking some leaves here and there likely won't have much impact on the local population. Some plants, however, aren't very abundant, or may even be endangered, so taking that handful of berries from the last specimen might mean wiping out the local population!

4. **Only take as much as you'll need.** As more and more people get into foraging, more and more of us are going to be out looking for wild ingredients, and that's awesome! So leave some for the

rest of us, ya greedy so-and-so. And, while we're at it, consider other local community members, too. Maybe only pick every third dandelion from the field so the local pollinators still have enough to feast on?

Correlative to 4: Know what you're going to do with something before you harvest it. Picking a bunch of plant material without leaving any behind is bad enough, but then letting it turn into green goop in your crisper because you don't know what to do with it? HAVE SOME DIGNITY, PEOPLE.

5. **Take your surroundings into consideration.** I've seen this a lot: articles on foraging that just encourage people to run out and start grabbing stuff from wherever. Did you ever stop to think, though, that there are better and worse places from which to collect wild edibles?

   As an example, suppose you're at a soccer game and see a lovely field of dandelions growing at the bottom of the field. You think, "those look tasty, and they're not on the field itself. Maybe I'll take a few...." BUT! Here is a Thing: dandelions have taproots. They burrow into the ground and suck up whatever is 6 inches below. Are you fairly confident that they haven't sucked up the pesticides used on the soccer field to keep it nice and green? If you're not, I wouldn't eat those dandelions if I were you. Picking some lovely nettles growing near a stream? Where does that stream originate? Picking some lambs quarters from a vacant lot? What was on that lot before it was vacant? These are important questions.

6. **Don't be a jerk to wild plants.** Don't be all ripping off their leaves, or tearing off their flowers, or cutting into their roots. Use clippers, and knives, and maybe consider keeping your clippers and knives and other tools clean so you're not spreading diseases around when you're cutting down different species. Just, be nice and have some manners, okay?

7. **Clean up after yourself.** This is especially important in more 'urban' wilderness areas, like parks and such—keep aesthetics in mind. Don't leave a bunch of plant clippings hanging around, or

big holes in the ground. Don't leave dirty plastic baggies on the trail, or sharp gashes in the plants in a park. And, finally....

8. Unless you're 100% sure you know what something is, DON'T PUT IT IN YOUR MOUTH. I'm repeating this because it's important.

Think of those rules as a kind of 'checklist.' Obviously, there are always exceptions, but generally speaking, if you follow those fairly simple guidelines, you're going to be able to collect wild ingredients in a way that has minimal negative impact on you and your ecosystem, and you'll be able to enjoy eating that dandelion salsa, or nettle dip, or chocolate-covered ginkgo leaves, as a participant in your local ecology. Good for you!

6 WILD FLAVOR: A MATTER OF "TASTE"

Picture iceberg lettuce. Everybody knows what it looks like and how it tastes, how the outer leaves tend towards the soft and green, and how the inner leaves are crunchy and sometimes sweeter. Whether cut into wedges and drizzled with Blue Cheese dressing, shredded in a machine and tossed into a taco, or layered on a burger or sandwich, the lettuce you grow in your garden or buy in the supermarket will consistently share these characteristics.

Iceberg lettuce (*Lactuca sativa)*, and its domesticated cousins like Romaine, share the **consistency of cultivation.** Through thousands of years of breeding, we can now fairly regularly assume that the iceberg lettuce we buy at the market will have the same flavor profile as the iceberg lettuce we order at a restaurant.

This tends to be true for most cultivated plants. A tomato will taste 'tomato-y,' and one variety of apple will taste similar to other examples of that variety, pretty much across the board. Cultivation allows us to control the qualities of these plants (although when we breed for one quality like color or shelf life, we often lose on other attributes like flavor).

Wild greens, however, are a different story entirely. Plants in the wild, impacted by a spectrum of influences and growing conditions, can vary in flavor, size, and color, sometimes significantly.

This can pose a problem for the home cook. If a recipe calls for, for example, a cup of chopped dandelion greens, and the cup of greens you happened to find the day prior were growing in full sun and relatively mature, they're going to be far more bitter than you may like, and will impact the recipe accordingly. For this reason, most recipes including wild ingredients should include "to taste" far more often than they do.

Wild lettuce (*Lactuca serriola)*, for instance—the common ancestor of all of our cultivated lettuces, can thrive in a number of conditions, all of which will influence its flavor. Most wild lettuces, members of the *Asteraceae* family, have an intensely bitter flavor profile. However, the experienced forager will occasionally stumble across an example that is mild and sweet. Consider: if no wild lettuces were ever mild and sweet, we would never have been able to breed these qualities into our domestic varieties!

Lactuca serriola
Image Source: Public Domain, https://commons.wikimedia.org/w/index.php?curid=1021227

If one is lucky enough to have stumbled across a sweet instance of wild lettuce without ever having tasted a bitter example, one is in serious danger of serving a *particularly intense* wild salad the next time!

Foraging groups online are full of debates on what the "true flavor" of wild edibles really is. Salal (*Gaultheria shallon*) is an excellent example. This Pacific Northwest understory shrub has edible berries. Those individuals who harvest salal from shaded areas report that the berries are "insipid" and good for no more than a trailside snack. Those collected from bushes growing in full sun, however, insist that salal berries are **actually** sweet and juicy and good for jams and pies.

They're BOTH right, of course! It's just that the growing conditions of each individual salal bush will determine the flavor profile of its berries.

Seasonality is another good example. Getting to know a wild plant means learning about how it manifests in all of the seasons. Something that can be used one way during one part of the year might be used differently earlier or later. This kind of deep, seasonal exploration allows us to interact with our plant companions on many levels. Someone who tastes a dandelion mid-summer may have an entirely different experience than someone who tastes the first dandelion greens of spring.

Really, the only way to know how a wild plant will perform in a recipe is to taste each single instance. It follows, however, that the experienced Finder will learn to determine what to collect based on her individual needs. A recipe calling for a bitter profile will benefit from wild lettuce instead of iceberg. Someone attempting a recipe for a sweet dessert made from salal berries should pick some from a bush growing in the sun, not from a bush growing trailside in a shady conifer forest.

7 WILD GREENS IN THE KITCHEN

When cooking with wild foods, here are a few things you may wish to keep in mind:

1. Clean those greens! Whether it's errant pollutants, unwanted insects, or a visit from the neighborhood dog, your wild foods should be cleaned before using. I soak mine for ten minutes in a bowl of water with a couple of tablespoons of plain white vinegar.

2. Wild greens can be notoriously bitter, especially members of the Asteraceae family like dandelions. Embrace the bitterness! Western culture doesn't appreciate bitter as a flavor, as we've been trained to like sweet tastes, so look at other cultures that use bitter ingredients and get ideas. Bitterness stimulates digestion and is an important gift of weeds.

3. Be creative! Just because a berry isn't sweet enough for a dessert doesn't mean you can't use it in a savory dish, or in a drink. Can't stomach that raw thistle? Why not juice it and add it to a smoothie?

4. **Think seasonings!** Wild foods sometimes have strong and unusual flavors that can contribute nicely to dishes in very small amounts.

5. Or, think bulk! Rather than tossing all of that chickweed into the compost or yard waste, why not blend it up and add it to a marinara sauce for an extra boost of vitamin C and flavor?

6. Experiment with pickles and ferments. Add dock to your sauerkraut, or dandelions to your kimchi!

7. Everything tastes good sautéed with olive oil and garlic—it's a great baseline method for figuring out something's flavor.

8. Some wild greens (the more delicate) don't store well. But, many do. The best way to store is to dunk in cold water, shake, and place in a zipper bag. Squeeze out the air and use a needle or safety pin to poke a few micro-holes in the bag. Keep them this way up to a week! (This works for store-bought greens, too.)

8 WILD EDIBLES: CULINARY KEYS

In light of the discussion in the previous chapters, it is worth noting that plant families do tend to have flavor profiles shared across their species, and plant parts have characteristics which, once known, can provide clues as to the kind of notes they will present in a dish.

It's safe to assume that a recipe calling for 'sweet' wouldn't generally benefit from the addition of thistle stalks (although who knows?).

With this in mind, and with the *caveat* that wild flavors can vary from individual to individual, we'd like to present the reader with a few keys that might assist the cook as she explores the wide variety of ingredients that can be found in the uncultivated landscape.

NOTE: The families listed in Table 1 contain examples from a variety of the most common families with edible members found in the wild. Almost all of these families also contain members that are toxic; just because a family is listed doesn't mean that members found therein are safe to consume.

The notable exception is the *Brassicaceae* family, in which all species are edible (though some, as they say, are more edible than others).

Table 1: FLAVORS BY FAMILY – GENERAL

FAMILY	FAMILY MEMBERS	FLAVORS/QUALITIES
Asteraceae (Sunflower family)	Dandelions, Thistle, Nipplewort, Chicory	Bitter
Brassicaceae (Mustard Family)	Garlic Mustard, Hedge Mustard, Lunaria, Bittercress	Sulfurous, sharp, biting
Chenopodaceae (Spinach family), ***Urticaceae*** (Nettle family)	Lambsquarters, Amaranth, Pigweed, Nettles	Mild, "spinach-like"
Polygonaceae (Buckwheat Family)	Dock, Japanese Knotweed, Lady's Thumb, Sheep Sorrel	Sour, mucilaginous
Malvaceae (Mallow family)	Mallow, Hollyhock, Linden Tree	Mild, mucilaginous
Rosaceae (Rose family)	Roses, Apples, Cherries, Plums, Various cluster berries, Hawthorne	Sweet, astringent
Ericaceae (Heather/heath family)	Salal, Madrone, Huckleberry, Blueberry	Sweet, slightly more sour than Rosaceae
Onagraceae (Primrose family)	Evening primrose, Fireweed	Slightly peppery, mucilaginous
Lamiaceae (Mint family)	Mint, Catnip, Dead nettle/Henbit	Strong, volatile

Table 2: USE KEY

1) **FLOWERS**
   a) Sweet
      i) Candied.
      ii) Salads.
      iii) Syrup.
   b) Mild, less sweet
      i) Quick pickles/relish.
      ii) Patties/fritters.
2) **FOLIAGE**
   a) Thick
      i) Slower, lower heat. Soups, stews, stir-fries, potherb ("an herb added to the pot!")
      ii) Best for ferments
      iii) Dock/mallow/plantain? Use to thicken soups/stews (mucilaginous)

   b) Thin
      i) Mild
         (1) Quicker, faster heat. Stir-fries.
         (2) Salads, pestos, garnishes.
         (3) Soups.
         (4) Dried as teas.
         (5) Use with eggs, chicken, fish.
      ii) Bitter
         (1) Quicker, faster heat. Stir-fries.
         (2) combine with sour/sweet for flavor balance, or cook in water and discard water to make milder.
         (3) Use with red meat, pork, fatty dishes.
3) **FRUIT**
   a) Sweet
      i) Jams, jellies, sauces, dessert
      ii) Candies
      iii) Syrups, drinks
   b) Mild/savory
      i) Syrups, drinks
      ii) Sauces, ketchup

4) **SHOOTS**
   a) Young, tender
      i) Cook as asparagus
      ii) Stir-fries
      iii) Peel, eat raw
   b) Older, Leafy
      i) Stir-fry
      ii) Pickle in vinegar
5) **ROOTS/RHIZOMES**
   a) Soft
      i) Boil, as potatoes
      ii) Thicken and sweeten
   b) Hard
      i) Roast, use in infusions

SOME "MASTER PREPARATIONS"

BASIC WILD GREENS SAUTÉ:

- Two parts wild greens (keep in mind they cook down and adjust accordingly)
- 1 clove chopped garlic per 2 cups greens (esp. for milder and bitter greens)
- Olive oil (NOT extra-virgin, which should only be used AFTER cooking is complete as heat destroys the flavors)
- Soy sauce/Liquid Aminos
- Sunflower Seeds (unsalted), 1 tbsp per cup of greens
- Salt and Pepper

Heat the olive oil on medium, one tbsp per cup of greens. Add the garlic and sunflower seeds and stir until aromatic, about 5 minutes. Add the greens. Stir until coated. Continue cooking until the greens are done to your liking. Thinner greens will require less cooking time. Add a tbsp of soy sauce/aminos, salt and pepper to taste, and serve.

ADD: Bacon, ham, etc.

BASIC WILD GREENS PESTO/SAUCE:

- One part wild greens
- ¼ part pine nuts/sunflower seeds/walnuts
- Chopped garlic, 1 clove per cup
- Olive oil, ½ cup extra virgin per 2 cups greens
- ½ cup sharp cheese (parmesan/romano)

Combine dry ingredients in food processor and process until minced. Slowly add olive oil with machine running. Add cheese and pulse a few times.

Use on Pasta, bruschetta, etc.

BASIC WILD FRUIT OR FLOWER SYRUP

- 2 parts water to one part berries/flowers/etc. by weight
- 1 part sweetener (sugar, honey, etc.)

In a saucepan, add berries/flowers/etc. and water. Bring to boil, then lower to a simmer. Cover **partially** with a lid. When reduced by ½, remove from heat and, using a cheesecloth or mesh strainer, drain as much liquid as possible into a bowl. Return liquid to the pan (solids can be discarded). Add sweetener, more or less depending on taste. More sweetener will preserve the syrup for a longer period. Warm until sweetener is incorporated.

Use in desserts, candies, drinks, etc.

9 WILD FLAVOR BY FAMILY: DANDELION CROQUETTES

One of the coolest things about being a forager is discovering new and interesting ways to use the delightful ingredients provided by your local biosystem. Since you're not paying "real money" for them, and since they're such an uncharted territory, "wild" ingredients really lend themselves to surprising and cool culinary experiments.

Case in point: everybody knows how amazing dandelions are, and they're one of the go-to easy greens for foragers, especially in the spring when the leaves are young and tender. The flowers can be made into wine, the roots are a good coffee substitute, &tc. &tc. &tc. But it appears the culinary virtues of this lovely plant are even more boundless than that. **For example, did you know that dandelion flower croquettes are amazing?!**

I have a yard full of dandelions, so procuring one cup of flower-heads was easy to do. You only want the flowers, and they should still be yellow and fresh. You don't want any stem or leaves.

Yes, it was a little tedious removing the petals from the bracts, but I think eliminating about 85% of the green stuff didn't impact the flavor negatively.

Most people tend to think of dandelions as bitter, but really it's just the greens. **Dandelions are members of the Asteraceae family, along with artichokes and sunflowers. Members of this family have flowers that emerge from relatively dense, flavor-packed receptacles (think artichoke hearts).**

The silky texture of the dandelion petals when combined with the flavors in the receptacle mingle into the perfect flavor and texture.

Add some bulk (I went with flour but the next batch will be experimenting with gluten-free options), add a binder (eggs), season accordingly (salt, pepper, garlic, oregano, chili powder for a kick, no onions), make into patties, and fry in a couple of tbsps olive oil until browned on both sides and cooked through.

For what it's worth, many of the plants in this family share these characteristics. Keeping this in mind allows for excellent kitchen fun, and gives you clues as to flavor profiles of other members of families. Maybe next time I'll experiment with thistle flowers, since they're also Asteraceae.

IN FACT, as another culinary treat, you could even try braised sunflowers!

Dandelion flower cross-section

10 PUTTING POTHERBS IN THEIR PLACE

from Hans Burgkmair, early 16th century

When you start dipping your toes into the stream of traditions encompassed by the word "foraging," one of the phrases that will come up most often is "can be used as a potherb." In all of the literature, however, rarely does one come across a decent explanation of just what a potherb *is*.

One might think that it's a plant that can be grown in a little pot, or a seasoning herb like basil or sage (insert obligatory Seattle 'pot herb' joke here, man). In fact, a potherb is any leafy green that can be cooked in a pot. "Cooked" is the key, here. Many potherbs would be too tough or bitter for a salad or sandwich, but added to a stew or soup? Excellent.

Potherbs make it super easy to incorporate wild foods into any dish you can think of. In many ways, it's reasonable, if you see the phrase "can be used as a potherb," to think "can be tossed into anything I'm cooking as an added vegetable."

HOWEVER!

Not all potherbs were created equally!

Remember, wild foods are ingredients, and wild potherbs often have different characteristics that will impact the way they're cooked. Knowing the family your potherb is in will give you a good idea of its culinary characteristics.

For example, last night's incredibly simple meal included two handfuls of lovely wild orache (*Atriplex spp.*—one of a few possibilities, but they're all edible to a degree):

This stuff is lambsquarters' mildly salty, slightly chewier cousin. It can be found around the tide-line on local saltwater beaches.

It's essentially the same as garden orache, which is in the spinach family (Amaranthaceae). The edible greens in this family tend to be delicate and "spinachy." As a "potherb," tossing it into a stew would result in losing the flavor of the leaves. Instead, I wilted it in a touch of olive oil and butter, and had it with feta over angel hair pasta (and a sprinkle of salal flower finishing salt):

It was sooooo good, and the preparation really allowed the plant to speak for itself as a star of the show.

I also recently harvested a lot of dock (*Rumex spp.*), one of my favorite wild edibles. Dock is a lot tougher than other wild greens, and can really take a nice, long, slow heating. Also, it's a member of the Polygonaceae family, which also includes sorrels, buckwheat, and rhubarb. This family tends to the sour, a keynote of interest when considering flavor.

The younger leaves are often still tender enough to prepare as the orache above, but the older ones can be leathery and bitter. With a

potherb like dock, you might add to a nice slow-cooked pork roast like this one:

There was nothing to it; I cleaned the dock, cooked the pork shoulder per usual (this works with any of your favorite pork shoulder recipes). Add two cups of chopped dock for the last hour of cooking. It'll break down nicely, and the result is AMAZING (and way more nutritious than if you just did the shoulder).

Our next potherb experience will be with common mallow (*Malva neglecta*). Most plants in the mallow family (Malvaceae, which includes okra, hollyhock, hibiscus, and durian) are edible. This particular plant is the common, weedy species. As anyone who has cooked okra knows, mallows also have an abundance of mucilage. The roots of the common mallow were originally used to give us marshmallows!

Since it's in the same family as okra, I went with the obvious: **gumbo**!

I don't have the time or wherewithal at the moment to do a full-stop actual gumbo dish, but the flavor combination came calling, and the thickening power of mallow turned this into one of my favorite dishes so far.

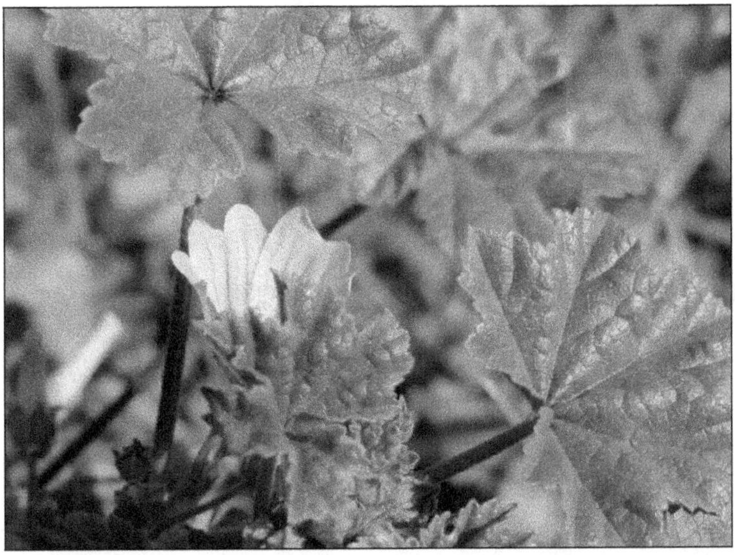

GUMBO-INSPIRED MALLOW AND DAISY RICE

Ingredients:

- One large bundle of mallow plants (stalks, leaves, flowers)
- Ten ox-eye or Shasta daisy leaves and flowers
- 2 cups chicken or pork stock (plus more as needed if liquid cooks down too much)
- 2 cans chopped tomatoes (with liquid)
- 1 cup frozen corn kernels
- 1.5 cups brown rice
- 5–6 links of your favorite sausage
- Pinch to handful of your favorite spicy pepper (I used some lacto-fermented jalapenos)
- 2 green onions, finely chopped
- 2 cloves garlic, finely chopped
- 1/4 cup fresh sage, finely chopped
- 1/4 cup fresh thyme, finely chopped

- 1/8 cup fresh oregano, finely chopped
- 1 bay leaf
- olive oil
- Salal flower finishing salt to taste
- Black pepper to taste

1. Clean the mallow and remove the leaves, flowers, and flower buds from the stems. Chop all but the stems coarsely. Tie the stems together with kitchen twine.

2. In a decent sized pot, add a couple of glugs of olive oil and turn to medium. When the oil is hot, add the onions, garlic, and spices (except the bay leaf). Stir until fragrant (about five minutes).

3. Add the mallow leaves. Stir until well coated and saute for another five minutes.

4. Add the stock, tomatoes, peppers, and corn. Bring to a boil.

5. When a boil is reached, add the rice, bay leaf, and mallow stems. Stir well, cover, and turn heat to low. Simmer for approximately 45 minutes (until rice is cooked).

6. Add the sausage, more water or stock as needed, and stir once again. Cover and let simmer for another 30 minutes, stirring occasionally and adding mroe stock/water as needed.

7. When the sausage is cooked through, add the daisy flowers and leaves.

8. Give another stir, cover and simmer for ten more minutes.

9. Remove mallow stems, remove from heat, and serve! Add hot sauce if that's your thing. Presentation-wise, you could top with some daisy flowers and petals and it'd look real nice. It also looks just fine all messy:

MMMMMMM……

This stuff is ***good.*** Like, make a batch and eat for lunch for days good. Like, invite friends and neighbors over to taste this amazing thing good. And it's all thanks to a scruffy lil' mallow plant!

11 "DECODING" WILD INGREDIENTS

"I don't think there are such things as bad ingredients that nature made, you know. It's just a matter of kind of taming it or decoding it. That's what we're doing, we're decoding our soil, our region."

-Rene Redzepi, "The Mind of a Chef"

Restricting your palette of wild ingredients to the "usuals," or to recipes in foraging books, can severely limit your options. If you really want to participate in your local biosystem through wild foods, there will come a point where the "cook like spinach" or "add to soups" may get a little boring.

Thing is, if you look far enough and are willing to experiment, there are so many flavors all around you that you might not realize are there until you've "decoded" them.

There are many plants around us that aren't toxic, but are also considered "inedible." Some of these are, in fact, not edible because they don't taste good or are too tough or or or, but often it's simply a matter of convention. Take, for example, cleavers, or bedstraw (*Galium aparine*). Most books on foraging will tell you that mature cleavers are inedible—perhaps good for tea, but too "sticky" and stringy to use in a dish.

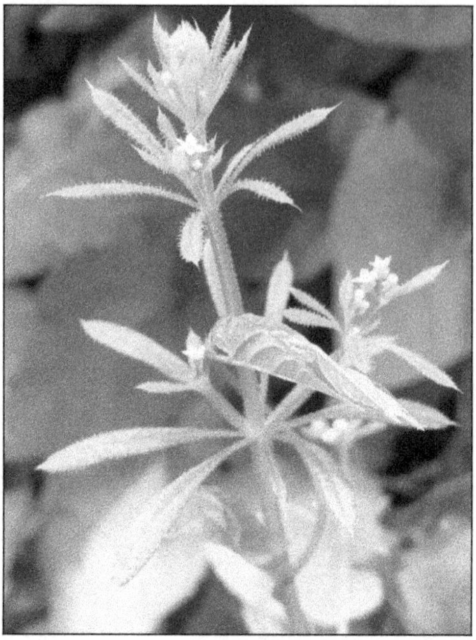

Cleavers (with friend). Note the sticky hairs!

It's true, you wouldn't want to eat a forkful of mature cleavers, but if you learn to ***decode*** them, you can develop different ways to prepare them that highlights their almost refreshing flavor and allows you to use them even at their most mature.

Since we're so unfamiliar with wild foods, it's easy to compare their flavors to what we already know. Lambsquarters "taste like spinach." Dock "tastes like sorrel." Many flavors we can discover in the wild, however, defy comparison once "decoded." Just as nothing "tastes like radish" but radish, so nothing tastes like (for example) the immature fruit of big leaf maple (*Acer macrophyllum*).

These are the samaras, or seedpods, that eventually turn into brown helicopters and flutter to the ground. Maple blossoms are a well-known wild edible, but few people know that the samaras can also be coaxed into edibility and have an incomparable taste that's well worth exploring.

Supposedly the hard seed inside can also be ground into flour in fall (a future experiment, for sure!).

In point of fact, maple leaves can also impart a flavor when used in cooking (though they're too tough to eat when mature). The indigenous people of the Pacific Northwest used big leaf maple leaves to wrap salmon for steaming, in the same way many cultures use banana leaves.

I don't have a great name for the recipe that follows, but experimentation helped me 'decode' the wild ingredients I discussed above. It's quick and simple, and massively delicious.

DECODED MAPLE PACKETS WITH CLEAVER PESTO PORK

Ingredients:

For the pesto

- Approximately 1.5 cups mature cleavers, blanched
- 2 cloves garlic
- 1/4 cup pine nuts or sunflower seeds
- 1/2 cup grated Parmesan cheese
- 1 tbsp salal salt
- approx. 3/4 cup olive oil

For the packets

- 1 lb ground pork
- 8 enormous big leaf maple leaves
- a handful of big leaf maple samaras

1. Cover the maple leaves in water and leave to soak for at least an hour. You could use some other liquid, but I wanted the flavor to come out.

2. Make the pesto. Chop the cleavers coarsely and add to a food processor with the garlic, Parmesan cheese, nuts/seeds, and salt. Pulse, gradually adding the olive oil until the consistency is smooth.

3. Mix the pesto into the pork.

4. After the leaves are done soaking, layer two of them in greased aluminum foil. Add about 1/4 of the pork mixture and top with maple fruit:

5. Fold the leaves over and wrap in the foil. Cook at 350F for approximately 45 minutes, or until internal temperature is 140F (I did these on a grill over indirect heat).

6. Remove, unwrap, and enjoy!

It's fantastic as-is, but would also be lovely on a sandwich or served with some kind of sauce.

12 WILD SEASONING

One of the biggest misconceptions surrounding wild foods is that they're stand-alones, or need a lot of preparation before they become usable in the average kitchen. However, with a little creativity and not a lot of work, wild ingredients can be just as versatile as standard grocery ingredients, and often far more interesting.

As an example, let's take Herb Robert (*Geranium robertiatum*).

Often considered an invasive, this attractive little geranium also goes by the more pejorative appellation "Stinky Bob." It does, indeed, have a strong odor when bruised or damaged, and, for this reason, when you suggest it's edible, even seasoned foragers will often decry its utility.

The fact is, however, that it's no more intense or overwhelming than cilantro or epazote (also shunned by the super-taster set). ***Yes, a salad***

made from Herb Robert would be overwhelming and fairly unpalatable. However, so would a salad made from cilantro! Instead of thinking of this plant as "gross," we can change our mindset to understand it as a flavor, and realize that using it sparsely can bring out subtleties of taste.

This is my philosophy for creating "wild finishing salts." In the interest of adding subtleties of flavor to cuisine, one of the best methods for doing so is by creating these simple seasonings.

The general approach is simple. Choose an ingredient, grind it as finely as possible, mix/grind with an equal part sea salt, and let dry.

Following this process results in some amazing flavors.

Top to bottom, the salts are made of spruce tips and lime zest, salal flowers and salmonberry, and Herb Robert.

Spruce tips and lime salt adds a citrusy zestiness, suitable for white meats like fish, chicken, and pork.

Salal flowers start off with an astringency that is followed by a delicate floral sweetness. This blend is excellent for rice, pasta, or even as a pinch on desserts.

Finally, the Herb Robert salt adds an excellent high note to Mediterranean or Latin American dishes (again, think cilantro). Sprinkled on falafel, a steak taco, or even *ceviche*, Herb Robert finishing salt will convert even the most virulent opponent of this little flower.

Remember: it's all about the flavor that surrounds you. If something is too strong, try using less!

There are small differences in approach between salts and sugars. Salt is a desiccant; it dries whatever it's mixed with. As such, it's often advisable to use fresh ingredients when making finishing salts, as they will provide much more of a flavor wallop as the salt absorbs the moisture.

Wild Ingredients for Finishing Salts:

-Any conifer needles (be sure to avoid harvesting the toxic yew)
-Sow thistle or other bitter green leaves
-Salal flowers
-Herb Robert
-Arbutus spp. Fruits
-Smoked tree barks
-Sumac (Rhus glabra) fruit

A nice finishing salt can also be made by simply smoking your salt with a native wood. Madrone-smoked salt in particular is one of our favorites.

Sugar doesn't desiccate as well; it's best to dry your ingredients and grind them prior to adding to sugar. The exception I've found to this is with the fruit of the Strawberry Tree (*Arbutus unedo)*, which becomes too hard to grind in a standard grinder when dried. Using fresh Arbutus is the way to go if you're going to make sugar.

Wild Ingredients for Finishing Sugars:

-Conifer needles
-Salal berries
-Strawberry tree/Arbutus spp. Fruits
-Hazelnut leaves/catkins

-Rosehips
-Sumac (Rhus glabra) fruit

Remember: it's all about the flavor that surrounds you. If something is too strong, try using less!

WILD "SPICE BLENDS"

One of the best ways to use wild ingredient throughout the year is to incorporate them into "spice blends," which can be used during cooking, to finish dishes, or even as rubs for veggies or meats destined for a grill or fryer. Again, experimenting with dehydrating/powdering and smoking does wonders. Experiment until you find proportions that work well for you.

"Lincoln Park" Herb Blend (makes about ¼ cup)

-Hazelnut (*Corylus cornuta*): 20 leaves (or so), dried
-Hazelnut: 24 catkin/cones, dried
-Hazelnut: 15 very small twigs, 1-2"
-Western Red Cedar (*Thuja plicata*): 1 tbsp "needles," chopped finely

Combine all ingredients in a small sauté pan and toast, on medium-low, until aromatic. Grind in a spice grinder. Sprinkle on chicken, fish, or vegetables.

Wild Ingredients for "Spice Blends"

-Native grasses
-Dock (*Rumex spp.)* seeds
-Plantain (*Plantago spp.)* seeds
-Dried leaves: Big leaf maple, hazelnut, blackberry,
-Large leaf Avens (*Geum macrophyllum)*: root, fresh or dried
-Bark: Alder, madrone, cedar, smoked or dried until brittle and grinded to a powder

13 WILD OILS AND VINEGARS

Fallen leaves and chilly temperatures don't mean you have to stop harvesting wild ingredients until Spring. No matter where you are or how cold (or warm) it is outside, there are always ample opportunities to experiment with new tastes, provided you know how to think about flavor. One of the nicest ways to experience wild flavor, and to prepare tasty foods using limited ingredients, is by infusing oils and vinegars.

When tasting wine, one is instructed to pay very close attention to flavors you might otherwise miss. Creating oils and vinegars with wild ingredients requires the same kind of discipline. We so rarely take the time to notice flavor, either because we're eating on the go or because we've become so used to the Western flavor palette that, with a few exceptions, the tastes no longer surprise us. Creating new flavors with wild, foraged ingredients allows us to once again experience surprise. This actually tastes like this?

Everything has a flavor. Don't be afraid to use ingredients like dead leaves, strips of bark, catkins, grasses, and seeds. Experimentation is key: keep a journal, and label your jars.

Consider the creation of wild infusions as similar as to that of perfume. Each ingredient has its own flavor profile. Is it sweet? Bitter? Tannic? Green? Mushroomy? Stack flavors in themes, so that two or three tastes complement one another. Perhaps your oil has a major heavy or tannic note; if so, play with sharper flavors like conifer or fir. Balance floral or fruity flavors with dusky fall leaves, or mild grasses.

Your base will always contribute flavor and qualities, which is well worth keeping in mind. Olive oil and coconut oil are wonderful, but their inherent flavors can mask the subtleties of wild ingredients. Apple cider vinegar is one of the best for infusion, but it does sweeten and flavor on its own. High quality unflavored vinegar is worth seeking out if you wish to create vinegar infusions that carry their own essence.

The Mad Forager's Kitchen

INFUSED VINEGARS

Infused vinegars can add a splash of flavor to salads, sauces, or sautés. They are also delicious when added to drinks; try a dollop in soda water for a refreshing treat.

INSTRUCTIONS:

1. Prepare your wild ingredients. Clean, then chop as finely as possible. If dried, pulverize to a coarse powder using a coffee grinder or blender. If fresh, use a sharp knife or food processor.
2. In a glass canning jar, add your wild ingredient. If dried, fill no more than three-quarters, as the dried material will expand. If fresh, fill to an inch or two below the rim of the jar.

INFUSION METHODS:

- Cold infusion: fill with vinegar, cover the mouth of the jar with wax paper to avoid corroding the metal lid, and set the jar in a dark location for 10–14 days. Shake daily.

- Hot infusion (use this method if you have bark or woody items in your blend): bring your vinegar to a boil in a small saucepan, then fill jar with boiling liquid. When cool enough to cover, cover the mouth of the jar with wax paper, seal, and set the jar in a dark location for 10–14 days.
- When infusion is complete, strain the vinegar using a cheesecloth lined potato ricer, or a wooden spoon/mesh strainer.
- Refrigerate, or store in a cool, dark, place.

PACIFIC NORTHWEST INFUSED VINEGAR RECIPES:

Forest Tree Vinegar #1

- Big Leaf Maple (*Acer macrophyllum*): 2 browned leaves with stems
- Hazelnut (*Corylus cornuta*): 5 leaves (or so), dried
- Hazelnut: 10 catkin/cones, dried
- Hazelnut: 10 very small twigs, 1–2"
- Western Red Cedar (*Thuja plicata*): Needles, fresh and chopped finely, ¼ cup
- Add vinegar to fill 1 pint jar

Conifer Vinegar

- Mix of needles, cones, etc. from Western Red Cedar, Douglas Fir, Western Hemlock, Grand fir, Pine, etc.
- Hot infusion works best.

Arbutus/Pine Vinegar

- Strawberry tree *(Arbutus unedo):* fruit, enough to fill ½ jar
- Pine *(Pinus spp.):* Needles, 1 c. chopped
- Pine: 3 small cones

- Madrone (*Arbutus menziesii*): bark, 2 palm-sized strips
- Add vinegar to fill 1 pint jar

INFUSED OILS

Infused oils are incredibly versatile; they can be used for everything from sautéing to dipping breads and crackers to adding flavor to cheeses or dressings.

Wild infused oils are particularly nice with lightly flavored foods: tofu, white fish, cheeses, chicken, etc.

INSTRUCTIONS:

- Prepare your wild ingredients. Clean, then chop as finely as possible. If dried, pulverize to a coarse powder using a coffee grinder or blender. If fresh, use a sharp knife or food processor.
- In a glass canning jar, add your wild ingredient. If dried, fill no more than three-quarters, as the dried material will expand. If fresh, fill to an inch or two below the rim of the jar.
- Fill with your chosen oil. Olive oil is great, but does add flavor. I prefer grapeseed or sunflower, as they are relatively inexpensive and don't have much flavor on their own. After initially adding the oil, use a chopstick to stir and allow the oil to settle. You may end up needing to add additional oil.

INFUSION METHODS:

- Slow infusion: set the jar in a warm location (i.e. in the sun, on a radiator, or a gas oven near the pilot light) for 10–14 days. Shake daily.
- Quick infusion: Place your jar in a saucepan, and add enough water that it comes up about three quarters of the way up the side of the jar. Turn the water to medium/medium high until it just starts bubbling (it should be between 100–150 degrees but no more). Leave at this temperature in the water bath for approximately an hour. At this point, you can remove and either strain for use or allow to infuse on top of the refrigerator for another 2 weeks or so.
- When infusion is complete, strain the oil using a cheesecloth/potato ricer, or a wooden spoon/mesh strainer. Allow to sit for 12 hours or so; if any water separates from the oil, you'll need to remove by pouring off the oil or using a gravy separator in order to avoid potential storage.
- Store in a cool, dark, place.

PACIFIC NORTHWEST INFUSED OIL RECIPES

"Seattle Parks and Rec" Oil

I found all of the ingredients in this oil in a local park. These ingredients should be available from late September—early November.

- Big Leaf Maple (*Acer macrophyllum*): 3 browned leaves
- Sow thistle (*Sonchus arvensis*): 7 green leaves (can substitute dandelion in a pinch, but these are sweeter)
- Queen Anne's Lace (*Daucus carota*): 3 flower heads, fresh or dried
- Clover (*Trifolium spp.*): 15 Flowers, entire
- Salal (*Gaultheria shallon*): 2 tbsp berries, dried
- Cover with grapeseed oil to 8 oz.

Forest Tree Blend Oil

These ingredients can be found year-round, with the possible exception of the Turkey Tail Mushrooms (*Trametes versicolor*), which can be dried when harvested or purchased from a reputable supplier.

- English Holly (*Ilex aquifolium*): Ten leaves, completely dried until no longer glossy, roasted at 250 degrees for 30 minutes, and ground to a powder
- Turkey Tail mushrooms (*Trametes versicolor*): Five coin-sized pieces, dehydrated
- Madrone tree (*Arbutus menziesii*): Strips of outer bark (approx. 1/4 cup)
- Alder tree (*Alnus rubra*): Hand-sized portion of outer bark, smoked, dried until brittle, and powdered

Large Leaf Avens Oil

A wonderful base oil. The Large Leaf Avens (*Geum macrophyllum*) can be identified in fall/winter by the persistent dried flower-heads, which resemble large burrs. This plant's roots have a distinct clove-like flavor.

- Infuse grapeseed oil with fresh roots and leaves (primarily roots) using Quick Infusion method above.

Geum macrophyllum ssp. perincisum

Large Leaf Avens

14 GET WEIRD WITH VEGAN "GRASSHOPPERS"

Have you ever wanted to:

- Have an exciting foraging food adventure?
- Indulge in a treat that's only available for about a week every year?
- Eat bugs without actually eating bugs?

The Spirit of Spring is creeping out of its cold and dreary hidey-hole (early, in most places). Here in the Pacific Northwest, this means crocuses (croci?) poking from the ground, robins making their annual appearance in our backyards, and leaf buds on the vast, pointy tangles of the "invasive" Himalayan blackberry (*Rubus armeniacus*).

Image via King County Noxious Weeds

Rather than pouring toxic awfulness onto plants that just happen to thrive where we don't want them, it's healthier for everyone to find ways to use the plants in question.

Everybody knows that blackberries are edible and delicious, but did you know the leaf buds that emerge in the Spring are also a tasty treat?

And here comes the adventure: find a blackberry bramble (reminder: make sure you know the plants haven't been sprayed or otherwise compromised). Now carefully insert a heavily gloved hand into a gnarled tangle of thorns, delicately popping the leaf buds off of the vine. This is potentially more painful than collecting the berries, but worth it. These little leaf buds are delicious cooked, and can be added to soups, salads, stir fries, or pickled like capers.

Or, you can try something more... *interesting*....

This season, I collected about 2 cups of blackberry leaf buds, in varying stages of 'emergence.' Looking at the form and texture of the leaf buds, they reminded me of... something. After a little consideration, I realized that these resembled in no small way the base ingredient in a lovely Oaxacan preparation called "chapulines": *edible grasshoppers.*

A fan of these guys, and a firm believer that eating insects is the Future of Food, I even happened to have a bag at the house:

What, I thought, if we could make vegan "chapulines," so that a) vegans and vegetarians could share in the edible insect experience, and b) the squeamish could enjoy the experience of eating 'bugs' without actually eating 'bugs,' and maybe get up the gumption to try the real thing?

Blackberries are in the Rubus genus of the Rosaceae family, so the leaves can be a little astringent. To "nip this in the bud," as it were, I soaked them in a mixture of soy sauce and water for two nights. This also served to add a little infusion of 'umami.'

Next, I rinsed them and dried them thoroughly.

I heated up some oil on medium high—not a ton of oil, just enough to cover—and added a batch of the blackberry leaf shoots, letting them fry in the oil for five minutes:

Sizzle sizzle pop

I scooped out the batch and placed them in a paper towel lined bowl to collect whatever oil wanted to drain off, then tossed them with:

- 2 tbsp salt
- 2 tbsp chili powder
- 2 tbsp 'sour salt' (citric acid—found in canning departments or Jewish food sections of any grocery store)—This is to replicate the lime traditionally used in fried chapulines; I was trying to avoid 'sogginess' that directly adding lime juice might cause. If you're not interested in using citric acid, you could also switch out for lemon pepper or be ok with lemon/lime juice.
- 1 tbsp cumin
- 1 tbsp garlic powder

(Adjust any of these to taste.)

This really looks like fried grasshoppers:

And they taste almost identical!

They have a nearly identical flavor, texture, and "mouth-feel" as the fried chapulines you can order as an appetizer at Oaxacan restaurants, and would be terrific with cold beer.

Even the resident vegetarian, typically grossed out by edible bugs, found them delicious.

For comparison, chapulines on the top row, vegan version below:

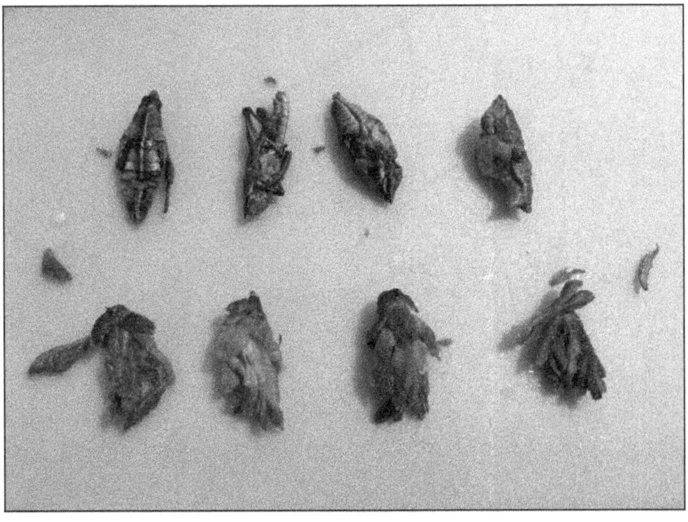

As I mentioned, these little guys are only available for about a week or two in the Pacific Northwest. Himalayan blackberry ranges throughout the Northwest and the Northeast, but theoretically this should work for most plants in the Rubus genus (blackberries, raspberries, etc.), if you can find them at just the right time.

More importantly, this recipe will have you thinking about foraging, food, using “invasives” as ingredients, and just how delicious fried things are, in entirely new ways. It’s yet another way to participate in your local environment.

Part Two:

A Parade of Plant Profiles

15 DANDELION

The humble dandelion has become something of the standard-bearer for edible weeds, likely attributable more to its ubiquity than its palatability. Thanks to the marketing budgets of herbicide companies and agricultural chemical concerns, it is also the most maligned example of the modern "weed."

In actuality, the dandelion is really a kind of horticultural bison, inasmuch as the entire plant can be used. After all, they were originally imported from Europe as food and medicine, and to provide forage for introduced pollinators.

Common name: Dandelion
Scientific name: *Taraxacum officinalis*
Family: Asteraceae
Other members of the family: Lettuce, artichoke, thistle, sunflower

Identification: Do you think it's a dandelion? It might be; then again, it might not. Dandelion has a number of closely related look-alikes, and although they're all generally interchangeable as far as culinary uses, some of this plant's cousins, like Cat's Ear (*Hypochaeris radicata)* and Hawksbeard (*Crepis capillaris)* can be slightly more bitter. It's worth knowing the difference.

The true dandelion has flowers on single, unbranched stalks which emerge from the center of a basal rosette of leaves. The leaves are deeply toothed, and smooth, not hairy.

Dandelions rest atop a deep taproot which is notoriously difficult to pull out. It can regenerate from a small portion of the root, so if you wish to remove the plant, you'll need to dig out around the entire underground portion very carefully.

"Taraxacum officinale - Köhler–s Medizinal-Pflanzen-135" by Franz Eugen Köhler, Köhler's Medizinal-Pflanzen - List of Koehler Images. Licensed under Public Domain via Wikimedia Commons

Where to find: Everywhere! Exercise caution, however, as dandelions are some of the most over-sprayed, chemical-saturated wild plants in the world. Be sure you know where your dandelions came from, and wash thoroughly before using.

When to harvest:

- **Flowers** when in full bloom, prior to seeding.
- **Stem** any time.
- **Leaves** when first emerging for salads/raw dishes, or any time for potherb/cooking.
- **Roots** prior to flowering if possible.

Uses:

- **Flowers** can be made into wine, or battered and deep fried as fritters. They can be added to salads and stir-fries.
- **Stems** can be eaten raw as a snack. They can be added to pestos, or chopped and added to salads and soups as garnish.
- **Leaves** can be added raw to salads when young and tender. They can be stir-fried or added to any stewed vegetable mix. They can also be added to pesto or salsa (recipe follows). If the leaves are older, you may wish to boil them very briefly in water to remove some of the bitterness.
- **Roots** can be peeled and cooked as a root vegetable if large enough, or added to stir-fries. They can also be roasted and ground to use as a coffee substitute (chicory is the more well-known member of the Asteraceae Family that has this quality).
- **The entire plant** can also be dried and made into a tea with tonic and diuretic properties.

DANDELION SALSA

Ingredients:

- About 1/4 to 1/2 lb. fresh dandelion greens, washed thoroughly and ripped into pieces.
- 6 oz. (or so) of fresh tomatoes or tomato juice.
- One sweet pear, cored, skin on.
- Three medium cloves of garlic.
- 1/2 of a medium yellow onion.
- 1/4 cup of lemon juice.
- 3 tablespoons of hot pepper sauce (tabasco et al), or to taste. Alternately, ½ jalapeno pepper, seeded, plus two tablespoons cider vinegar.

Instructions:

Puree everything together in a blender or food processor and serve cold with tortilla chips. SIMPLE AND DELICIOUS

16 NIPPLEWORT

When teaching a foraging class, nipplewort is one of the plants most likely to elicit cries of, "is THAT what that is?" Very common and widely distributed, nipplewort is also very easy to identify due to its unique leaf pattern.

About the funny name: according to most sources, the closed flower buds resemble nipples, hence the nomenclature. Apparently it was widely cultivated as a vegetable in ancient Rome, and is common in "wild greens" mixes use in the kitchens of Europe (e.g. Greek *horta*). Its flavor profile is slight, mildly bitter; in texture it is chewier than lettuce. In some ways, it resembles a kind of 'tofu' of wild greens, inasmuch as it takes on the flavor of whatever one prepares with it.

According to a 1987 study in the journal *Economic Botany,* nipplewort is high in extractable oil, and may be a useful renewable energy source sometime in the future.

Common name: Nipplewort
Scientific name: *Lapsana communis*
Family: Asteraceae
Other members of the family: Lettuce, artichoke, thistle, sunflower
Identification: Nipplewort is one of the easiest wild greens to identify due to the unique secondary lobes found on its lower leaves:

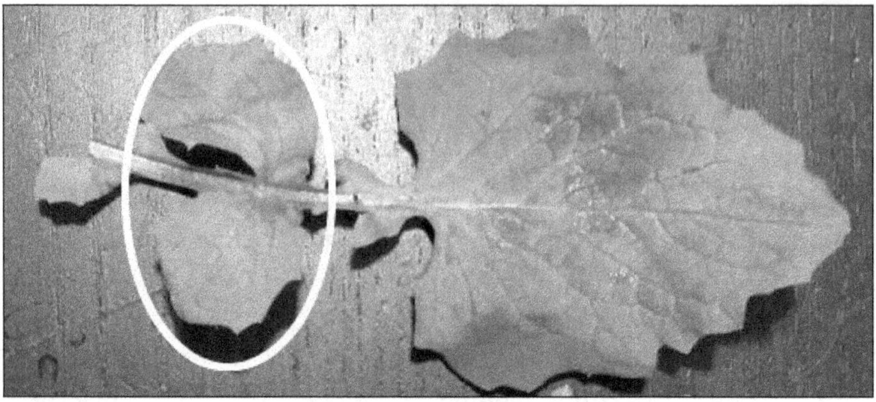

The leaves are alternate, emerging from a basal rosette when young, and displaying a variety of shapes as the plant grows.

When more mature, but prior to bolting and flowering, nipplewort displays a noticeable "bulk" and can become quite bushy for an herbaceous plant. After bolting it becomes tall and branched, displaying small yellow dandelion-like flowers on multiple stems:

"Lapsana Communis Habitus" by Christian Fischer. Licensed under CC BY-SA 3.0 via Wikimedia Commons

Where to find: Forests, woods, edges, gardens, roadsides, parks. Nipplewort prefers full sun to dappled shade. A prolific and dispersive plant, it is typically found in large stands/communities.

When to harvest:

- **Leaves** when first emerging for salads/raw dishes, or any time for potherb/cooking.
- **Flower buds** prior to flowering.

Uses:

- **Leaves** can be added raw to salads when young and tender. They can be stir-fried or added to any stewed vegetable mix. They can also be added to pesto or salsa (recipe follows). If the leaves are older, you may wish to boil them very briefly in water to remove some of the bitterness.
- **Flower buds** can be collected *en masse* and brined in vinegar and spices as a caper-like condiment.

WILTED LAPSANA WITH YUM NOODLES

Ingredients:

- Approximately one pound nipplewort leaves. Don't bother with the little leaves at the top of the plant. You want the thicker, lobed leaves towards the bottom.
- Four cloves of garlic.
- Three tablespoons of sesame oil.
- Two tablespoons of soy sauce.
- One tablespoon of raw sugar.
- Two cups of your favorite noodles.
- Garnishes like toasted sesame seeds, chopped scallions, and umeboshi.

Instructions:

1. Make a couple of cups of your favorite noodle. Soba is good, as are any standard wheat-based or gluten-free noodles. When the noodles have finished cooking, rinse with cold water and set aside.
2. You'll want to get as much of the stem off of your leaves as possible. Be sure you have a lot of nipplewort! This stuff cooks down like you wouldn't believe.
3. Soak your leaves in water with a couple of tablespoons of vinegar mixed in for about twenty minutes. This'll help clean the leaves and mitigate any little bitterness left in them.
4. While the leaves are soaking, mince the garlic. Add the sesame oil to a sauté pan and turn to medium high.

5. Drain the nipplewort and squeeze out any excess liquid.

6. When the garlic starts sizzling (about 3–5 minutes), add the nipplewort to the hot pan. Stir it as it cooks until it becomes wilted and delicious looking (about 5 minutes).

7. Add the soy sauce and sugar. Continue stirring for another five minutes.

8. Dump the whole thing onto the noodles. Add garnish: toasted sesame seeds, chopped scallions, chiffonaded *shiso*, even crumbled bacon.

9. YUM!

17 CHICKWEED

Chickweed: *so pernicious, yet so delicious*! It's well-known as a common foe for many home gardeners, but shouldn't be. Its delicate flavor and delightful crunch make it a notable favorite for foragers (and their chickens!). It spreads quickly, but its roots are shallow, which means it can provide a lot of herbaceous food without disturbing the other members of a garden community.

This low-profile, matting plant also creates an excellent ground cover that blocks out many other "weeds" (if that's a concern for you). It is typically available in milder climates year-round, and can also be found in open woods and park spaces. There are a few different chickweed species, and all are edible, but we focus on the "common" version here.

Chickweed is incredibly high in Vitamin C, and makes an excellent salve for treating skin conditions like eczema.

Common name: Common Chickweed
Scientific name: *Stellaria media*
Family: Caryophyllaceae
Other members of the family: Baby's breath, bladder campion

Identification: A matting, low-profile plant. Chickweed has multiple stalks that emerge from a single root system, quickly spreading to cover an area:

Chickweed in a Seattle garden bed

The leaves are opposite with entire margins (non-serrated/lobed). A single line of hairs runs along the stem, 'spiraling' at each node. If the stalk is pulled apart, an inner core emerges, especially in younger plants.

Chickweed flowers emerge from finely haired buds at the terminal end of each step. The flowers are white, and star-shaped (thus "Stellaria"), with 5 divided petals (resembling 10!):

Chickweed in flower. Licensed under CC BY-SA 3.0 via Wikimedia Commons

POISONOUS LOOK-ALIKE: Spotted spurge (*Euphorbia maculata*). Once you know the difference, it's difficult to confuse the two. Spurge has milky sap and different flowers. Don't eat spotted spurge.

Where to find: Gardens, lawns, parks. Chickweed prefers full sun to shade, but can also be found in dappled woodland areas.

When to harvest:

- **Whole plant:** Any time. More tender when young; stems may need to be removed due to toughness when older.

Uses:

- **Whole plant** is excellent raw in salads when young and tender. They can be stir-fried or added to any stewed vegetable mix. They can also be added to pesto or made into a bouillon (recipe follows).

CHICKWEED PESTO

Ingredients:

- 2 cups chickweed.
- 1-2 cloves garlic (to taste).
- ¼ cup sunflower seeds.
- 3/4 cup olive oil.
- ¼ cup grated hard Italian cheese (pecorino, romano, etc.).
- Salt & pepper to taste.

Instructions:

1. In a food processor or blender, pulse all of the ingredients except ¼ cup of the olive oil and the cheese until smooth.
2. Pulse the remaining oil and cheese into the mixture immediately prior to serving.
3. Serve over pasta or rice, or use as a dip.

GATHERER'S BOULLION

Ingredients:

- Foraged greens (esp. chickweed, dandelions, nipplewort, lambsquarters, dock, etc.).
- Garlic.
- Salt.
- Pepper.

Instructions:

1. Clean the greens.
2. In a food processor, add ¼ cup salt, 1 tsp. pepper, and one clove garlic, per 2 cups of greens.
3. Process the ingredients until very fine. Remove and squeeze in a cheesecloth until no more liquid comes out.
4. Spread the mixture very thinly (1/4 inch) on a dehydrator screen and dehydrate according to instructions. OR:
5. Spread very thinly (1/4 inch) on a baking sheet and bake at 180 degrees until dried (about 1 hour).
6. Add one teaspoon per cup of hot water for a quick broth, or use as a base for soups.

18 PLANTAIN

And you, Plantain, mother of herbs,
Open from the east, mighty inside.
over you chariots creaked, over you queens rode,
over you brides cried out, over you bulls snorted.
You withstood all of them, you dashed against them.
May you likewise withstand poison and infection....

— Anglo-Saxon 9 Herb Charm

I remember first encountering plantain (*Plantago spp.*) in a Florida outfield, where I'd been exiled due to a lackluster interest in little league baseball. Its flowers extended six inches or so above the ground, waving in the breeze like tentacled creatures from some ethereal place.

*English Plantain (**P. lanceolata**) flower. Image by Kurt Stüber [1]—caliban.mpiz-koeln.mpg.de/mavica/index.html part of www.biolib.de, CC BY-SA 3.0*

Little did I know at the time that this humble and ubiquitous plant had so many uses, and would prove to be one of the tastier wild greens!

Native to Europe, where the Saxons considered it one of the "Nine Sacred Herbs," there is a dark side to plantain as a signifier of imperialism. Essentially, plantain is spready. Its seeds are mucilaginous (more on that in a minute), which allows them to cling and survive. One of the first naturalized European stowaways, it soon became so abundant in North America that some indigenous communities refer to it as "white-man's footprint."

The two most abundant species you'll find in your neighborhood are Plantago lanceolata (lance-leafed, narrow, ribwort, or English plantain) and Plantago major (broadleaf, or common plantain). It's easy to tell the two apart, and they're often found growing right next to one another.

Plantain has been recognized since at least the time of that Anglo-Saxon charm above as an excellent general medicinal, especially for external scrapes and bruises. The entire plant can be used as a poultice or in a salve.

Taken internally, the seeds (aka "psyllium seeds") are especially useful for adding "bulk" to help digestion. They can be added to meals directly, or powdered and added to baked goods, or even stirred into smoothies. *AS A MATTER OF FACT, you can buy a mixture of sugar, "orange flavoring," and powdered plantain seeds for $15 at your local grocer's: everybody's favorite "Daily Fiber Therapy," Metamucil.*

Next time, just make your own. The seeds of broad-leaf plantain dry on the stalks; strip, grind into powder, and use.

In my experience, the broad-leaf plantain is the nicest for eating. If you collect the leaves when young, you can add them directly to salads and stir-fries (see "potherbs"). The older leaves require the removal of the ribs (or a willingness to deal with a little stringiness).

Common name: Plantain
Scientific name: *Plantago spp.*
Family: Plantaginaceae
Other members of the family: Penstemon, Hebe

Identification: A small, herbaceous perennial. Flower stalks emerge from a basal rosette, leaves either lance-shaped or ovoid. The leaves have thick, parallel venation.

Flower heads are spikes—conical in lance-leaf, lanceolate in broad-leaf. The flowers tend to be white/green/brown and are very small, clustered on each spike. Each plant can produce thousands of seeds.

POISONOUS LOOK-ALIKE: Spotted spurge (Euphorbia maculata).

Where to find: Gardens, lawns, parks.

When to harvest:

- **Whole plant:** Any time. More tender when young; leaf veins may need to be removed due to toughness when older.

Uses:

- **Whole plant** is excellent raw in salads when young and tender. They can be stir-fried or added to any stewed vegetable mix. They can also be added to pesto or made into "chips" (recipe follows).

Broad-leafed plantain

Lance-leafed plantain has…lance…shaped…leaves……….

PLANTAIN CHEESE CHIPS

Ingredients:

- 10 or so enormous broad-leaf plantain leaves

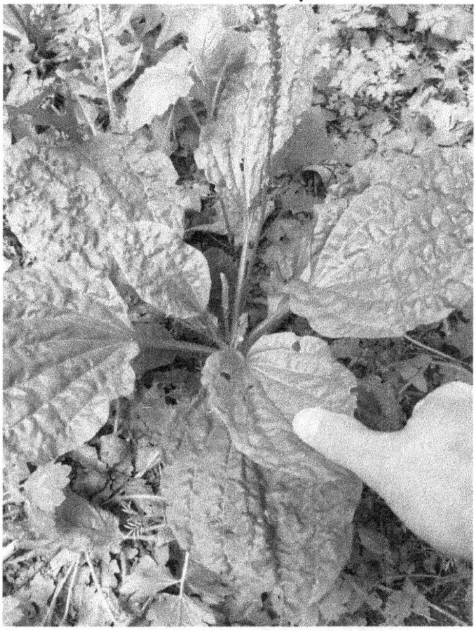

They should be bigger than your thumb

- Cooking oil (olive is nice)
- Your favorite cheese, shredded, approx. 1 cup
- Finishing salt to taste

Instructions:

1. Pre-heat oven to 375F.

2. Clean your plantain leaves. For all wild greens (especially those found in the dreaded DOG PEE ZONE), I recommend submerging in a mixture of water and a few splashes of white vinegar for at least 10 minutes, swishing around occasionally.

3. Dry the leaves thoroughly. Use a paper towel.

4. (Optional.) De-rib the leaves. It seems like it would be tricky, but there's a method. Pinch the base of the leaf, where the stalk meets the leaf itself. Gently wiggle until the very base of the leaf snaps all the way around. Grasping the leaf in one hand, slowly pull the stem away from the leaf. The majority of the ribs should pull out of the leaf.

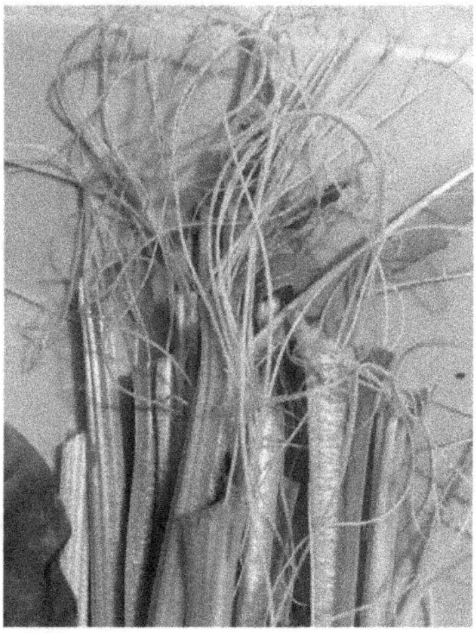

5. On a cookie sheet, lay out leaves so that none are touching (you may want to do multiple batches). Brush each leaf in oil. Flip, then brush the other side.

6. Place in the oven for six minutes. The leaves should already be mostly crispy:

7. Flip and sprinkle each leaf with about a tablespoon of cheese. Place back in oven for three minutes.

8. Sprinkle with finishing salt, and serve!

9. You can do this with any wild green, but the nice thing about these leaves is how large they are. You can even add more toppings if you like—the ones pictured below have some chopped spinach, too.

No matter which way you use it, plantain is definitely a wild plant that should be in your bag of tricks.

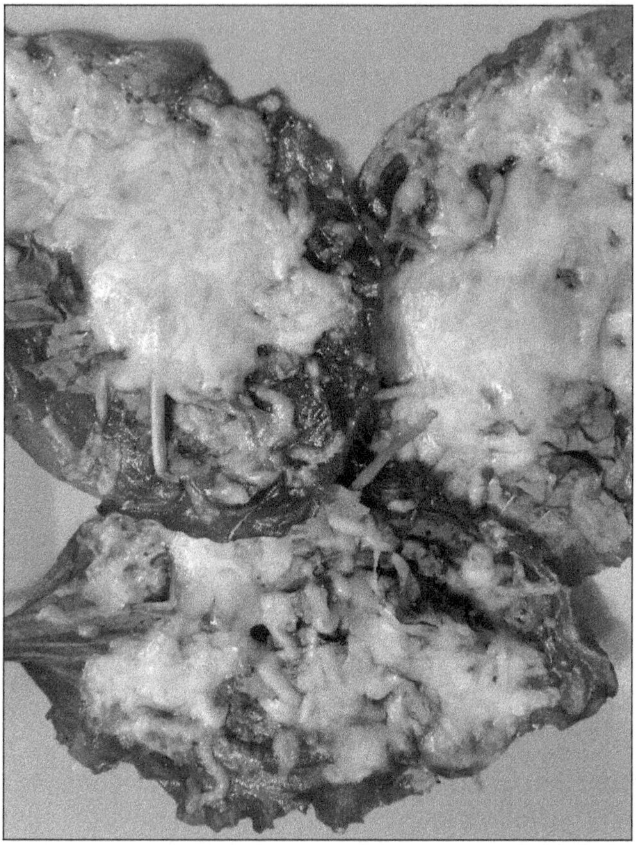

19 LAMBSQUARTERS

Do you like spinach? If so, you'll love lambsquarters, which are to common garden spinach as wild venison is to factory-farmed beef. In fact, lambsquarters are known in many places as "wild spinach," and are closely related to both the domesticated bagged green stuff you find at the supermarket and other members of this family like beets and chard and quinoa.

Also known as fat hen, pigweed, or goosefoot, these plants typically mature in mid-to-late summer, just in time for the pagan festival known as "Lammas," thus its most common moniker.

Lambsquarters contain oxalic acid, often declared a 'risk' when gathering wild foods, and worth discussing.

A WORD ON OXALIC ACID

Oxalic acid gives many greens their distinctive sour flavor, and most foraging guides will recommend eating these foods in moderation. The fact is, a large number of vegetables commonly consumed also contain high levels of oxalic acid; determining levels of oxalic acid content and the harm it causes is often difficult and depends in a large part on the conditions in which the plants in question were grown.

Typically, moderate consumption of these foods is perfectly fine for healthy people (the major exception being rhubarb leaves). It would take Herculean consumption levels to result in toxicity for most people. However, those with kidney conditions or gout should avoid these foods. For more information we recommend oxalicacidinfo.com.

It's also worth noting that lambsquarters are particularly inclined to sucking up heavy metals and poisonous nitrates from the soil. For this reason, plants growing in construction sites or industrial areas should not be harvested.

That said, none of the above should keep the enterprising

gatherer from enjoying this delicious plant when found in the wild and harvested safely.

Common name: Lambsquarters, pigweed, goosefoot
Scientific name: *Chenopodium album*
Family: Chenopodiaceae
Other members of the family: Spinach, beets, quinoa
Identification: Mature leaves are lightly toothed, diamond to lance-shaped, covered in a "dust." The undersides of the leaves are silver-white and shiny.

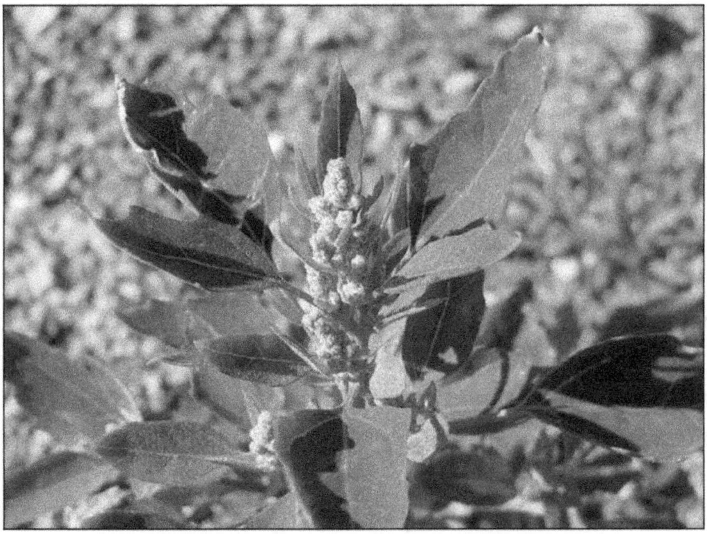

"20140812Chenopodium album" by AnRo0002 - Own work. Licensed under CC0 via Wikimedia Commons

As the plant grows, it branches and spreads like a candelabra. Clusters of seed-bearing, non-showy flowers emerge from the ends of the branches.

POISONOUS LOOK-ALIKES:

- **Epazote (Teloxys ambrosioides).** Epazote leaves don't have the powdery-white shininess of lambsquarters, and the plant smells resinous. Epazote is a common seasoning in Mexican cuisine, but shouldn't be eaten in quantity due to its toxicity.

- **Nightshades (*Solanum spp.)*.** Some weedy nightshades can resemble lambsquarters at certain stages of growth. These are typically hairy, with showy flowers and berries presenting at mature stages.

Where to find: Gardens, vacant lots and fields, parks. Sunny areas. Edges.

"20120819Schwetzingen16" by AnRo0002 - Own work. Licensed under CC0 via Wikimedia Commons

When to harvest:

- **Leaves:** Any time, but larger leaves are more useful. Branch tips can be collected whole when least woody. Found late July-September.
- **Flowers/seeds:** Any time when present.

Uses:

- **Leaves** excellent raw in salads or cooked as a green.
- **Flowers/seeds** can be milled or used as a grain like quinoa. Flowers can also be made into patties or fritters.

CHENOPOD CROQUETTES with BEET-CREAM

BEET CREAM:

Ingredients:

- 3 m sized beets, greens attached
- ¾ c heavy whipping cream
- 3/4 tsp salt

Instructions:

1. Preheat oven to 400 degrees.
2. Clean beets, removing tops. Reserve greens for later use.
3. Wrap beets lightly in foil. Roast for approx. 50 minutes, or until fork-tender.
4. Remove from foil, let cool, and remove skin from beets (should peel off easily w/a paper towel or spoon).
5. Quarter beets and add to blender with cream and ½ tsp salt, adding cream ¼ cup at a time until smooth. Chill for ~1 hr.

***CROQUETTES*:**

Ingredients:

- 2 c. quinoa OR lambsquarter seeds, pre-cleaned/soaked
- 3 tbsp + ½ c. olive oil
- 4+ c. water
- 1 c. lamb's quarters, packed

- 3 garlic cloves, chopped
- 3 green onions, sliced
- 1.5 tbsp soy sauce or tamari
- 3 m-l eggs
- 8 oz chevre/goat cheese
- 3 tbsp lemon juice
- 2 tbsp black pepper
- 3 tbsp Szechuan peppercorns, crushed (opt.)
- Reserved beet greens

Instructions:

a) MAKE THE SEEDS

1. Add 1.5 tbsp olive oil to a large saucepan. Set burner to medium high. When oil is hot, add quinoa/lambsquarter seeds and stir until slightly browned, about 5 min.

2. Add water, bring to a boil, immediately lower to simmer and cover. Cook for 20 minutes or until soft and fluffy.

b) MAKE THE GREENS:

1. Over medium low heat, sweat the garlic and onions for 5 minutes.

2. Add lambsquarters and soy sauce, raise heat to medium, cover and continue cooking until soft, stirring occasionally, approx. ten minutes.

c) MAKE THE CROQUETTES:

1. When quinoa and greens are done cooking, mix together and let cool.

2. When cool enough to touch with the hand (but not before!) add the eggs, cheese, lemon juice, pepper. Mix thoroughly.

3. Form into patties approx. 6 inches in diameter. If too crumbly, another egg may be added.

4. Heat the remaining olive oil in a sauté pan over medium heat and fry croquettes until browned on one side, then flip and do the same on the other side. Transfer to a paper-towel covered plate.
5. While croquettes are cooking, steam the beet greens for 10 minutes.

d) FINISHING TOUCHES:

1. Serve each croquette topped with beet greens and a spoonful or two of the cream. **Bon appétit!**

20 BITTERCRESS

You likely know hairy bittercress by its more common moniker, “shotweed.” This little guy flowers well into Autumn in temperate climates, and can be found year-round in areas with light snow cover—a good plant to look for when gathering winter greens. Once done flowering, it emits numerous tiny seedpods. Even the softest touch against these seedpods will result in an explosion of tiny projectiles as the plant shoots its offspring into the world, thus its common appellation.

This dispersive habit makes it a well-known “enemy” of people who don’t like “weeds,” but this is an awesome plant--very flavorful--which can also provide a useful ground cover in garden beds.

Bittercress is in the *Brassicaceae* family, along with many of our favorite vegetables like broccoli and cabbage. It contains the same sulfuric compounds that give radishes and mustards their ‘kick,’ though bittercress is slightly milder, sometimes no more spicy than arugula (and almost never actually “bitter”). Every now and again, however, you’ll run across an example that opens the sinuses and delivers the punch of wasabi.

Common name: Bittercress, shotweed
Scientific name: *Cardamine hirsuta*
Family: Brassicaceae
Other members of the family: Broccoli, cabbage, mustard, radishes, watercress

Identification: Hairy bittercress presents as a rosette with pinnately compound leaves, then emerges into a bushier low herb as it matures.

" Cardamine hirsuta plant" by Rasbak - Own work. Licensed under CC BY-SA 3.0 via Wikimedia Commons

Tiny, white flowers, with the four part "cross-shape" indicative of *Brassicas* ("cruciferous" plants), bloom from the terminal end of soft stalks. The flowers eventually mature into soft seedpods which gradually harden. Brushing against the hard seedpods releases the seeds into the air, sometimes as far as a few feet from their progenitor.

POISONOUS LOOK-ALIKES: Butterweed/groundsel. In its basal rosette stage, butterweed (*Packera glabella*), a toxic member of the Asteraceae family, can resemble bittercress. Bittercress smells mustardy/peppery. Butterweed leaves are also toothed/serrate, where bittercress leaves are not.

Where to find: Gardens, lawns, parks, woodlands.

When to harvest:

- **Whole plant:** Any time prior to seed development. Leaves, stems, and immature seedpods when soft/tender. More tender when young.

Uses:

- **All aerial parts of the plant** are excellent raw in salads when tender. They can be stir-fried or added to any stewed vegetable mix. They can also be made into pesto or used in herb blends, sauces, or dips.

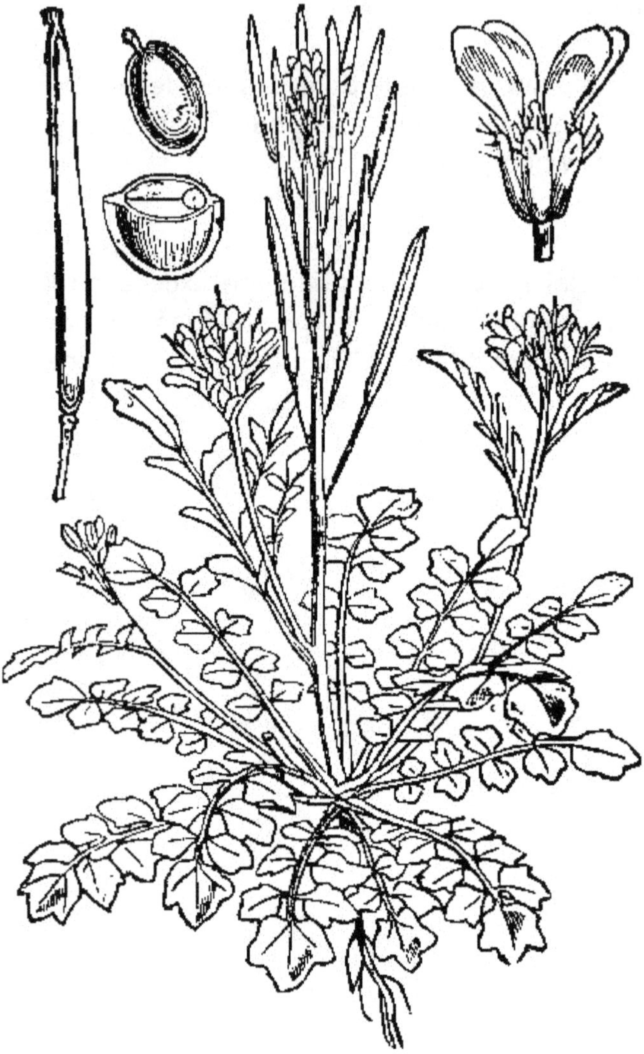

"Nsr-slika-178" by Martin Cilenšek - Scan from Naše škodljive rastline (1892). Licensed under Public Domain via Wikimedia Commons

SHOTWEED RICE

An excellent, *pilaf*-inspired side-dish which can be made into a main course with the addition of a protein.

Ingredients:

- 1 cup hairy bittercress, minced.
- 1 cup white rice.*
- 2 cups vegetable or chicken broth.
- 1 clove garlic, minced.
- ¼ cup sunflower seeds.
- 3 tbsp olive oil.
- Salt & pepper to taste.

**Brown rice or other grains may be substituted—increase liquid and cooking time accordingly.*

Instructions:

1. In a saucepan, heat the olive oil on medium until a wooden spoon placed in the oil produces bubbles.
2. Add the sunflower seeds, garlic, and rice. Increase heat to medium high and stir until rice begins to turn golden.
3. Add bittercress, salt, and pepper, and continue stirring until cress has wilted.
4. Add broth, mix to incorporate, and bring to a boil. Immediately cover and lower the temperature to low.
5. Simmer until rice is cooked, approximately 15-20 min. for white

rice (45 min. for brown rice, also increase liquid by 2/3 cup).

6. Mix, fluff, and serve with butter!

21 BROAD-LEAVED AND CURLY DOCK

Dock is incredible! You've seen broadleaf dock (*Rumex obtusifolius*) or curly dock (*Rumex crispus*), but you probably didn't know what it was called.

"Rumex-obtusifolius-foliage" by Sten Porse - Licensed under CC BY-SA 3.0 via Wikimedia Commons

It's all over the place in abandoned lots or along sidewalks or inside city parks, all waving around its leaves like a bunch of red-veined banners, sitting there contentedly being related to buckwheat and sorrel and whatnot.

If you dig into foraging literature, you'll likely come across a few descriptions of dock: pick the leaves while they're really young, they'll say. It's too bitter to enjoy, they'll say. Don't eat too much because of all of the—GASP—Oxalic Acid, they'll say (see *Wild Flavor Vol. 1* for a discussion on oxalic acid). Well folks, dock is a delight, and it works really well as both a potherb, a soup green, and a wrapping for dolmas. YUM!

Common name: Dock (Curly, Broad-leaved, Yellow)
Scientific name: *Rumex crispus* (Curly), *Rumex obtusifolius* (Broad-leaved) .
Family: *Polygonaceae*
Other members of the family: Buckwheat, rhubarb, sorrel, sheep sorrel, Japanese knotweed,

Identification: Herbaceous perennials with leaves emerging from basal rosettes. Central stalk produces additional alternate leaves and branches containing flowers/seeds.

Leaves: **CURLY:** Lanceolate, regular margin with distinct curling edges. **BROAD-LEAVED:** Wider leaves with non-curling edges. Both have leaves that gradually unfurl from center of plant as it grows. Older leaves may become spotted/mottled.

"Rumex crispus15052006rosette" by Henry Brisse
Licensed under CC BY-SA 3.0 via Wikimedia Commons

Flowers: Green-red with no petals. Clustered on top of stem branches in large numbers. Flowers brown as they mature, producing abundant seeds.

Fruit: Seeds.

Stem: Large stalk grows from center of rosette.

Height x Width: 3 ft. x 2 ft.

"20130702Ampfer St Arnual1" by AnRo0002 - Own work. Licensed under CC0 via Wikimedia Commons

POISONOUS LOOK-ALIKES: Docks can resemble the incredibly deadly Foxglove (*Digitalis spp.)* when young/in the rosette stage. Foxglove leaves are "softer" looking, and have veins that run up the center of the leaf, almost parallel. **Even a small portion of foxglove can be deadly, so be 100% sure you know it's dock prior to harvesting.**

L: foxglove R: dock

Where to find: Moist/wet areas, stream banks, waste areas, shorelines, parks.

When to harvest:

- **Seeds** when dried on the stalk late in the season (fall through winter).
- **Leaves** when first emerging (spring, then after the first frost) for salads/*horta*, when younger and still tender (spring/summer) for potherbs, when older (year-round) for *dolmas*.
- **Stems** when still tender.

Uses:

- **Seeds** can be ground and used for texture in crackers/baked goods. They can also be sprouted.
- **Leaves** can be added raw to salads when young and tender. They are best when still curled in the center of the plant's rosette. They make an excellent addition to mixed cooked greens, particularly in recipes which also include tomatoes (think gumbo, jambalaya, etc.). You may wish to boil briefly in a change or two of water if your particular find is too bitter or too sour. When older, leaves can be added to *hortakopita* in the spring. When very old, large, and tough, leaves can be used to make *dolmas*. (Recipes follow.)

BROADLEAF DOCK DOLMAS

Ingredients:

FOR THE WRAPS:

- 10–15 broadleaf dock leaves. You could also use curly dock, if you're so inclined, though it'd be more difficult to stuff 'em since curly dock leaves are... curly. Try to harvest older, tougher leaves for this, not the younger ones. A few spots are okay, but you're stuffing them, so avoid big holes or tears. Clean them well, trying not to tear them.

- 1/8 cup sea salt
- 2 cups water

FOR THE STUFFING:

- 1 ½ cups cups white rice
- 3 cups vegetable broth
- ½ cup sunflower seeds
- 2 cloves garlic, minced

- 2 tbsp lemon juice
- 2 tbsp olive oil
- Salt and pepper to taste

FOR THE DOLMAS:

- 1 ½ cups veggie broth
- Paprika to taste

Instructions:

BRINE:

1. Heat up the water, dissolve the salt, let cool. Drop the leaves into the brine and refrigerate for at least 3 days.

STUFFING

1. In a sauce pan, sauté the rice, garlic, and sunflower seeds in the olive oil over medium heat until golden.
2. Stir in the remaining ingredients and bring to a boil. Immediately lower to simmer and cover. Let cook for 15 minutes, then allow to cool.

DOLMAS:

1. Remove leaves from brine and rinse briefly.
2. Remove the end stems and cut the larger ones in two.
3. Place about a tablespoon and a half of stuffing into each leaf, and roll them up like little burritos (burritoitos?). It's difficult to avoid overstuffing them—err on the side of less filling per leaf.

4. Arrange in a sauté pan, packed fairly tightly. Add broth (veggie or chicken) and sprinkle with paprika. Cover and simmer for 1/2 hour or until the leaves darken.
5. Serve and eat.

You could make an argument for serving them with sour cream for dipping, or even tzatziki, but they're perfectly delightful just on their own. The leaves are mildly sour with a hint of bitterness that adds to the complexity of the dish.

HORTAKOPITA

Ingredients:

- 3 cups mixed wild greens (adjust for flavor between bitter/sweet/sour), cleaned and chopped coarsely
- Filo dough (frozen is fine, or if you want to make it, go for it)
- 3 cloves garlic, minced
- 2 tbsp olive oil + more to taste
- 2 tbsp lemon juice
- 1 ½ cup feta cheese, crumbled
- Salt and pepper to taste

Instructions:

1. Preheat oven to 300F.
2. Add olive oil to sauté pan on medium heat.
3. When oil is warm, add garlic until aromatic.
4. Add the greens, lemon juice, salt and pepper. Stir frequently until wilted and remove from heat.
5. Coat the bottom of an 8 x 10 baking dish with olive oil, and layer with filo dough. Add greens, feta, dough in layers until dish is full.
6. Brush final layer of filo with ample olive oil.
7. Bake for 20 minutes. Serve hot or cold.

22 FIREWEED

When people think of the Pacific Northwest, they generally think of wet, overcast, rainy weather. This is true for much of the year, but between June and October, our climate actually tends towards dry, drought-like conditions, often accompanied by wildfires.

During fire season, the smoke makes for some lovely sunsets:

Wildfire season also brings out the local *Epilobium* species. On a weekend drive to a campsite, the fields and roadsides will appear coated in enormous stands of *Epilobium angustifolium*.

A pioneer species, fireweed colonizes disturbed or disrupted environments.

"Pink-purple wildflowers and subalpine fir trees near the Jarbidge River in the upper Jarbidge River Canyon in Nevada, Nevada" by Famartin - Own work. Licensed under CC BY-SA 3.0 via Wikimedia Commons -

It's called "fireweed" because after a forest fire, it's usually one of the first plants to sprout in burned areas. Pollinators and butterflies love fireweed, and, when in flower, stands of *Epilobium* often buzz and shimmer with life.

It's also an incredibly useful and quite tasty wild edible!

You can use pretty much every part of this plant. The shoots can be cooked like asparagus. The flowers and young leaves can be eaten raw; they're slightly sweet, and very mildly astringent. The stems, when older and thick, can be peeled and enjoyed as a snack. The older leaves can be cooked as a potherb, as can the flowers, and act both to flavor and to thicken soups/stews/etc.

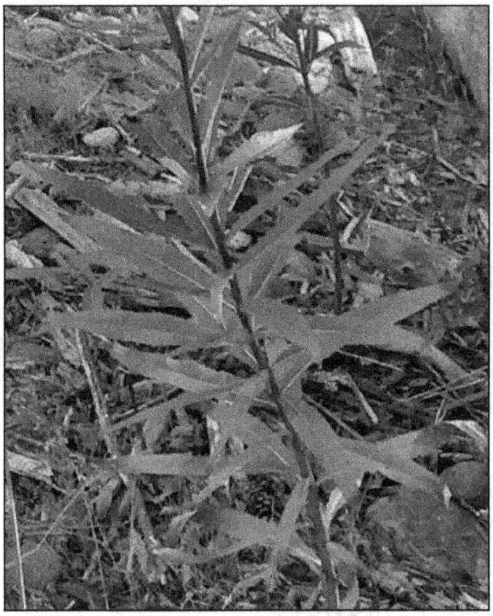

Fireweed's range isn't limited to the Pacific Northwest. It's found all over the Northern Hemisphere from Canada down to California, with the exception of the Central and Southeast U.S.

This awesome plant is a great demonstration that even in hot, dry, drought-like conditions, there is food everywhere you look.

Common name: Fireweed, great willow-herb, rosebay willowherb
Scientific name: Epilobium (Chamerion) angustifolium
Family: *Onagraceae*

Other members of the family: Evening primrose, Fuchsia

Identification:

A perennial, *E. angustifolium* is unmistakable when in bloom in summer and fall. Lance-shaped leaves spiral alternately up the 4-7 ft. tall brownish stalk, culminating in a cone-shaped spike of pinkish-purple flowers. The blooms progress up the plant; the lowest flowers are the youngest. The flowers have four separate petals and 8 distinct stamens.

Given that a single fireweed plant can produce up to 80,000 seeds, it is commonly found in stands and can cover entire fields.

When not in flower, the leaf is the easiest way to identify the plant. The leaf veins don't traverse the leaf all the way to the edge; instead, they loop just before the edge and form together.

POISONOUS LOOK-ALIKES: None significant.

Where to find: Edges, open fields, clear-cuts, prairies, meadows, roadsides. It usually grows in full sun, but can tolerate some areas of dappled shade. When late in the season, it may be possible to find younger *Epilobium* still in flower at higher elevations.

When to harvest:

- **Shoots** in spring when first emerging.
- **Leaves** when young for salads/raw dishes, mature but still pliable for potherb/cooking, older for tea.
- **Flowers and buds** any time when present.
- **Stem** when young and pliable for cooking/pickling. Can be

peeled and eaten later in the season.

- **Roots** spring through fall.

Uses:

- **Shoots** can be eaten raw or cooked like asparagus.
- **Leaves** can be eaten raw when young, cooked when mature, and dried and/or fermented as tea when mature or older. A fairly well-known tea is made in Russia from fireweed.
- **Flowers and buds** can be eaten raw or added to syrups or confections. Fireweed honey is very popular.
- **Stem** can be eaten raw, cooked, or pickled.
- **Roots** can be mashed or used as a starch; they should be peeled to remove some of the bitterness.

FIREWEED "CHIMICHURRI"

Ingredients:

- Approximately one pound fireweed leaves. Young stalks are OK too, as long as they don't contain woody bits.
- ½ medium sweet onion.
- One clove of garlic.
- 1-3 chiles depending on your heat preference.
- ¼ c each of chopped cilantro, oregano.
- ¾ cup extra virgin olive oil.
- ½ cup apple cider vinegar.
- ½ cup lime juice.

Instructions:

1. Blend all of the ingredients together in a food processor. Add more liquid to taste as necessary depending on consistency of fireweed leaves.
2. Use as a marinade for red meat or serve as a sauce. Also tasty over noodles!

23 STINGING NETTLE

Stinging nettle: the ***gateway drug*** for many a forager. There's something stimulating and exciting about collecting and eating a plant we were warned about as children. It's not often we have to pay for our food with potential pain, but the flavor and other benefits of dining on wild nettle cause many of us to turn a blind eye to its sting.

Mention stinging nettle in a group of people used to eating them, and prepare for rapturous expressions of joy.

In the southern United States, the name "stinging nettle" is often applied to the native *Cnidoscolus stimulosus*, or spurge nettle, a white-flowered herb with a far more painful effect. Although the latter does have edible roots, we refer here to *Urtica dioica*, which ranges more generally in cooler climes (though can certainly be found in pockets of the South).

Nettle has also been used, historically, as a source of fabric, cordage, and medicine.

Thomé, Flora von Deutschland, Österreich und der Schweiz 1885

Common name: Stinging Nettle
Scientific name: *Urtica dioica*

Family: *Urticaceae*

Other members of the family: Ramie, Gympie-gympie

Identification: The easiest way to identify stinging nettle is by accidentally brushing up against it. Tiny, hair-like stingers made almost entirely of formic acid line the stems and leaf-bottoms.

As the stingers are almost entirely hollow crystalized chemical, anything from friction to mild heat will dissolve them and make them safe for consumption.

If stung, a quick poultice made from plantain or dock will bring almost immediate relief.

Leaves: Opposite, simple with serrate margins. Can be heart-shaped.

Flowers: Non-showy, emerging from the axils (where the leaf meets the stem), clustered on threads.

Stems: Green, square-shaped, herbaceous, becoming more woody with age.

Height x Width: 4-5 ft. x 1-2 ft.

POISONOUS LOOK-ALIKE: White Snakeroot (Ageratine altissima). These plants are very similar until the flowering stage. White snakeroot doesn't have stinging hairs, and when in flower, its white blossoms appear at the top of the plant, a dead give-away.

***There are anecdotal reports that nettles harvested after flowering may cause kidney damage. Although the author hasn't found any scientific evidence to back up this claim, it's best to err on the side of caution.**

Nettles should also be avoided by pregnant women for the same reason.

Where to find: Forests, stream-banks, parks, "waste" areas, edges, wet areas, often half-way up-slope from water.

When to harvest:

- **Leaves:** Early spring – mid summer. Best when young, but the entire tops can be harvested at any stage in its growth.
- **Seeds:** Mid – late summer. After flowering, the threads at each axil will be covered in seeds. The seeds can be stripped and collected.

Uses:

- **Leaves**: Excellent wilted or added to stir-fries or as a potherb when young. Pesto. Tea, when dried, medicinally.
- **Leaves and young stalks**: Soups, smoothies.
- **Seeds**: Fresh, reportedly as a stimulant.

STINGING NETTLE DIP/SPREAD

Excellent for dips or spread onto a sandwich, this is an easy way to use nettle at any stage in maturity.

Ingredients:

- 2 cups Stinging nettles
- 1 16 oz package cream cheese
- 1 clove garlic
- ½ tsp sea salt
- ½ teaspoon white pepper
- Instructions:

1. Fill a large bowl with ice and water.
2. Bring a large pot of water to a boil. Drop the nettles into the water and blanch for 3 minutes. Using tongs or a slotted spoon, transfer the nettles to the ice water.
3. Drain, squeezing out as much liquid as possible (liquid may be reserved and used as tea/broth if you're feeling saucy!).
4. Chop nettle coarsely.
5. Place ingredients in food processor. Pulse until well combined. Serve chilled.

STINGING NETTLE FLAVOR BOMB

A note on the recipe: since you never know how much nettle you may find, the instructions will be proportional instead of by specific amount.

Ingredients:

- Stinging nettles
- Water (1 cup per cup of nettles)
- Salt
- Agar (powdered or bricked)
- Any other deliciousness you'd like to include

Instructions:

1. Add approximately one cup of water per cup of nettles to a pot, and bring to a boil. When water is boiling, add nettles for approximately three minutes.
2. Remove nettles and retain water in pot.
3. The nettles should no longer be sting-y. Remove woody stems and chop coarsely.
4. Return nettles to the water. Bring back to a boil, then reduce to a simmer. Cover, and let simmer for 20–30 minutes, until water is dark green.
5. Pulverize agar if not already powdered (a coffee grinder works well, but ripping it up seems to work just fine, too). I use about 0.25 oz per cup of water. It's ok to play around with the ratio; more agar results in a more solid final product.
6. Add the agar plus salt, about 1 tsp per cup of liquid, to the nettle mixture. (At this point, you can also add other delicious ingredients if you're looking to create a bouillon or insta-soup. Pepper, garlic, onion , bay leaves— whatever your palate fancies.)
7. Stir, then let simmer an additional ten minutes or until agar is completely dissolved.
8. Remove from heat and put into a container. Place in fridge. After a few hours, depending on how much agar you used, you should have something that's the consistency of a jelly, or even a solid brick. If it's not solid enough for you, reheat and dissolve

more agar into the mix.

And that's it! The final product is a super-concentrated nettle explosion. The agar and salt will preserve it, refrigerated, for a couple of months.

A bowl of nettle soup in a soy sauce dish

Use it sparingly in savory dishes. Add a tablespoon to a mug of hot water for a yummy nettle broth. Toss a spoonful into the cooker next time you make rice for extra nettle oomph. This little flavor bomb trick will satisfy your spring nettle flavor yearning and amaze your friends!

24 HEDGE MUSTARD

Hedge mustard (*Sisymbrium officinale)* is technically considered an "invasive weed," but it's really a SUPER good plant to have. You can eat the leaves (spicy!), make "mustard" from the flowers and seeds, and that "off." in its name, short for "officinale," indicates that it was considered Important Enough for Linnaeus to name after the place where medieval monks would keep their medicine.

Wild brassicas are incredible, and everywhere. I had this enormous hedge mustard in my yard:

I'd never seen one so big. It was almost PULSING with life-force. It'd established itself in the pictured concrete block, and I wonder if the shelter of the block helped it germinate by shading it just so and collecting just the right amount of moisture (*note to self—try growing brassicas in concrete blocks in next year's garden*).

Bees and other pollinators loved my enormous hedge mustard.

Like all wild brassicas, hedge mustard has slightly spicy, tangy leaves, best when young but edible even in older stages. Found very widely distributed in habituated areas, hedge mustard is just as happy in the shade as it is in the sun.

Common name: Hedge mustard, wild mustard

Scientific name: *Sisymbrium officinale*

Family: *Brassicaceae*
Other members of the family: Domestic mustard, radishes, broccoli, cabbage, cauliflower

Identification: Annual. Emerges as rosette in spring. Can be bushy or stalked depending on conditions.

By AnRo0002 - Own work, CC0, https://commons.wikimedia.org/w/index.php?curid=22342507

Leaves: Alternate, pinnately lobed. Generally triangular. Terminal leaf lobe often hastate (arrowhead-shaped).

Flowers: Small, yellow, terminal in clusters at the end of stalks which curve upwards. Parts of four per Brassicaceae family pattern (four petals, four sepals).

Fruit: Pods. Usually haired, running closely parallel to stem. Later in season,

Stems: Green, square-shaped, herbaceous, becoming more woody with age.

Height x Width: 4-5 ft. x 1-3 ft. depending on conditions

POISONOUS LOOK-ALIKES: None significant.

Where to find: Vacant lots and fields, parks. Edges.

By Dermorgendanach - Own work, CC BY-SA 4.0, https://commons.wikimedia.org/w/index.php?curid=40671821

When to harvest:

- **Leaves:** Any time. Younger are more tender. Older can be spicier/more bitter.
- **Flowers/buds/seeds:** Any time when present.

Uses:

- **Leaves** excellent raw in salads when younger and tender, or cooked as a green. Wonderful added to lactofermented preparations.
- **Flowers/buds/young seed pods** taste like mustardy broccoli. Excellent pickled. Can also be used raw in salads or added to stir fries.
- **Seeds** can be milled and used as a spicy condiment.

Sisymbre officinal. Sisymbrium officinale Scop.

By Amédée Masclef - Atlas des plantes de France. 1891, Public Domain, https://commons.wikimedia.org/w/index.php?curid=5771188

HEDGE MUSTARD VINEGAR

This is a spicy treat, well suited to hot summer days!

Ingredients:

- 1 1/2-2 cups hedge mustard leaves, buds, and/or flowers (and or seeds depending on season)
- 1 tsp dill
- Raw, unfiltered apple cider vinegar

Instructions:

1. Chop hedge mustard coarsely. Add dill and mix.
2. Place in a sealable, non-reactive container.
3. Cover with vinegar. Place in refrigerator and allow to mature for 48 hours to one week depending on desired strength, shaking the container once daily.
4. Strain the vinegar & reserve. The hedge mustard can be added to a salad or stir-fry or used as a relish.
5. The vinegar can be used as a salad dressing, or in recipes, or added to a Bloody Mary or other savory mixed drinks.

25 OX EYE DAISY

Out of all of the weedy surprises that the author has discovered, Ox Eye Daisy (*Leucanthemum vulgare)* greens are one of the finest. Not only are they intensely and pleasantly flavorful—a kind of spinach-meets-green-pepper—but they're also prolific, and can (and should!) be added to the roster of wild staple greens whenever in season.

The flowers can also be eaten, raw or cooked, and daisy buds can be included on the list of caper-like condiments when pickled.

Ox Eye Daisies are a tried-and-true insect repellent, with especial efficacy (according to folklore) against fleas. They are also well-regarded as divinatory oracles ("He Loves Me, He Loves Me Not").

It's worth noting that almost all of the daisy species are edible—even the tiny lawn, or English daisy—but as Ox Eyes are the most common, this is the species we'll focus on.

Common name: Ox Eye Daisy, Marguerite

Scientific name: *Leucanthemum vulgare*

Family: *Asteraceae*

Other members of the family: Dandelions, artichokes, sunflowers

Identification: Ox Eye Daisies are easy to recognize when in bloom, with their cheery white and yellow ray flowers surmounting the terminal ends of its stems. The flowers first appear as tight round buds. Each flower sits atop a 1'-3' tall stalk, which can be traced back to a central stalk emerging from the center of a basal rosette.

Once you become familiar with the smooth, dark-green leaves of the Ox Eye Daisy, you'll be able to pick them out even when in the rosette stage prior to stalk emergence. The lower leaves are oval to lance-shaped with rounded lobes, often appearing "toothed." Leaves grow narrower as they alternate up the stem.

POISONOUS LOOK-ALIKES: None significant.

Where to find: Gardens, lawns, parks, meadows, pastures.

When to harvest:

- **Whole plant:** Any time. More tender when young. In milder climates, leaves may be found year-round.
- **Flowers** are typically present from early spring through summer.

Uses:

- All aerial parts of the plant are edible.
- **Flowers** can be stir-fried or added to any stewed vegetable mix. They can also be battered and deep-fried, or added raw to salads.
- **Flower buds** can be pickled in vinegar and used as a condiment.
- **Leaves** can be cooked as pot-herbs/mixed greens. They can be clipped directly from the basal rosette at any stage.

DAISY-DILLAS

The green pepper meets spinach flavor of daisy greens makes them excellent for inclusion in Mexican-inspired dishes, like these quick and easy quesadillas.

Ingredients:

- 2 cups Ox Eye Daisy greens, young stems, and flowers, coarsely chopped.
- 1-2 cups shredded cheese (cheddar or pepper-jack are nice!).
- 4 – 6 flour tortillas (depending on how 'stuffed' you want your daisy-dillas).
- 1 clove garlic, minced.
- 3 tbsp olive oil.
- Salt & pepper to taste.

Instructions:

1. In a saucepan, heat 1 tbsp of the olive oil on medium. Add the garlic and stir until it becomes aromatic.
2. Add the daisy and sauté until wilted. Remove from heat.
3. Add the remaining olive oil to a large sauté pan. Turn to medium. When the oil has a slight sizzle, add one of the tortillas.
4. After 1-2 minutes, add ½ cup of the cooked greens and ½ cup of the cheese to the top of the tortilla, spreading evenly. Cover the pan.
5. After 1-2 minutes, just as the cheese begins to melt, add a second tortilla to the top of the first and press down slightly so the cheese adheres. Flip and cover again.
6. 1-2 minutes later, or when the quesadilla is slightly brown on the bottom, remove to a plate.
7. Repeat steps 3-6 with remaining ingredients. It may be necessary to add 1 tsp of olive oil to the pan between each quesadilla.
8. Serve with sour cream or plain yogurt, tomato salsa, guacamole, etc.

26 CONCLUSION

What Happened When I Foraged My Vegetables For A Month?

It gave me a SUPER-POWER!

During the month of June 2017, I attempted what I refer to as the WILD FOOD CHALLENGE:

The general idea was to try to replace as many of the plants as possible in my diet with wild, foraged, and found ingredients.

It wasn't easy!

I didn't succeed in the one-to-one replacement I'd hoped for. Instead of using wild ingredients in every meal, I'd say I had about a 3/4 success rate, but I'll take it.

It may have been simpler if we lived in a more rural location, but since we live in the city, foraging options are more limited. However, this very limitation led me to develop a new kind of super power. When you work with a fairly small palette of ingredients, you really develop the skill to decode the flavors in your environment.

You begin to appreciate more subtle flavors, and to develop new ways to extract them (I'm now a HUGE fan of wild seasoning salts).

You learn to create recipes that are templates instead of specific methods of preparation, and to find interesting ways to use greens based on their characteristics even if you're not completely sure how they taste.

Once you start getting into plants and their uses, you will never be bored again.

In many ways, foraging allows you to use "cheat codes" to "level up" your involvement with your surroundings. This is a kind of super power; now when you walk into a park or the forest, you start "seeing" like some kind of Lego Master Builder. You no longer suffer from "plant blindness" and instead you develop a real kind of Second Sight!

Don't just take my word for it, though: get outside and find out for yourself. There's no more interesting way to involve yourself in your surroundings, to participate in your local biosystem.

INDEX

Recipes in BOLD

INVIRONMENT

Food, Farming & Environment

"Serving the Life Force. Making the Inner like the Outer. Eating and Growing."

http://medium.com/invironment/

Invironment is an online publication dedicated to food, farming and the environment. Specializing in long-form articles and short ebooks, we publish topical pieces related to the inner and outer worlds and their intersections. Invironment is edited by Jeremy Puma (http://www.pumaculture.com), a permaculture and wild foods instructor in Seattle, and Tim Boucher, a small organic farmer in Quebec.

www.ingramcontent.com/pod-product-compliance
Lightning Source LLC
Chambersburg PA
CBHW060833110426
R18122100001BA/R181221PG42736CBX00014BA/1
* 9 7 8 0 6 9 2 0 9 5 4 4 7 *